LETTERS TO ARCHITECTS

FRANK LLOYD WRIGHT

Selected and with commentary

by

Bruce Brooks Pfeiffer

The Press
at
California State University, Fresno
Fresno, California 93740

To Olgivanna Lloyd Wright who, at her husband's side for thirty-five years, shared his work, his hardships, his triumphs, and his life dedicated to the Cause of Architecture.

ACKNOWLEDGMENTS

For permission to use the photographs in this volume, my grateful thanks to the following:

Pedro Guerrero: 60 Years of Living Architecture, Exhibition; Frank Lloyd Wright and Exhibition Workmen.

Hedrich-Blessing: Taliesin; Annunciation Greek Orthodox Church.

S. C. Johnson & Son, Inc.: Johnson Wax Buildings.

Fred Lyon: V. C. Morris shop, interior view.

George McCue: Louis H. Sullivan, Wainwright Building.

Sylva Moser: A Musical Evening at Taliesin, Christmas, 1924.

William H. Short: Frank Lloyd Wright at the Guggenheim Museum.

The Frank Lloyd Wright Memorial Foundation: for all remaining photographs used in this volume.

Quotations from Frank Lloyd Wright, *Genius and the Mobocracy*, Duell, Sloan and Pearce, 1949, are reprinted by courtesy of the copyright owner, The Frank Lloyd Wright Foundation.

Quotations from Frank Lloyd Wright, *An Autobiography* are reprinted by permission of the publisher, Horizon Press, from *An Autobiography* by Frank Lloyd Wright © 1977, New York and by permission of the copyright owner, The Frank Lloyd Wright Foundation.

My especial thanks to architect Philip Johnson for permission to use several of his letters to Frank Lloyd Wright; to Henry-Russell Hitchcock for permission to reprint his September 19, 1952 letter to Frank Lloyd Wright; and to Lewis Mumford for permission to reprint his critique of Fallingwater.

The cover photograph is taken from a 1937 portrait by Helen Morrison and is the only extant one of its kind. It is reproduced by courtesy of Mrs. Frank Lloyd Wright.

CONTENTS

PREFACE

We who studied with Frank Lloyd Wright at Taliesin always called him "Mr. Wright." When he spoke to us, his apprentices, he addressed us by our first names, reflecting respect on the one hand and affection on the other. Because I knew him during the last ten years of his lifetime as Mr. Wright, it would now, some twenty-five years later, be impossible for me to refer to him, write about him, or speak of him, with any other name than that which I employed during my first decade at Taliesin.

For the most part the letters in this volume are addressed to architects practicing throughout the world, many of them contemporaries with Mr. Wright during the first half of the twentieth century. To give a broader insight into the development of his work, a group of letters to critics has been included. Taken as a whole, this selection of letters aims at revealing an underlying unity of purpose: the growth of his work and the unquestionable magnitude of influence it engendered in the world of architecture.

As early as 1909 Frank Lloyd Wright recognized himself as the founder of a new architecture, which he would call Organic Architecture. During a lifetime that surpassed six decades of creative work, he gave to architecture shapes and forms virtually unmatched in this or any other age. He considered it the sacred obligation of the architect to build for mankind buildings which were appropriate, natural, and above all beautiful in relation to whatever situation they were to find themselves.

Organic Architecture, as Mr. Wright practiced it, observed a deep reverence for the individual and placed him lovingly in harmony with nature and the features of the landscape. All that he designed or built was guided by that principle, and his undeterred allegiance to it is continually manifested in the letters he wrote throughout his life. Those letters are a testimony to his work and to his constant crusade in the cause of architecture. Architecture was paramount in his life, but he did not separate work from life: the two are irrevocably interwoven in him and in all he did.

The five groupings of letters that follow convey what it meant to be responsible for so lonely an undertaking, so profound an accomplishment. He once clarified the significance of the early years of his career in a letter to a critic saying, "You start your piece as though there was a crew taking the initial ride. No. Not so. LHS [Louis H. Sullivan] and I began an era. Alone. Don't start me with a crew. I had a head start and the crew that came along after has only yet partially realized what it all meant."

As the most prolific innovator in the entire realm of architecture he was destined to stand alone among his contemporaries. The very nature of his genius placed him in that isolated position. But it would be completely erroneous to describe him as a "lonely" man. He was a man rich in personal friends and acquaintances all around the world. Nevertheless he would fight with those friends, sometimes fiercely, to defend his work and the principles it upheld. These letters from his own hand follow the turbulent course of his life work, at first ignored in his native country and often misunderstood abroad, but finally recognized and honored the world over. He was fortunate enough to outlive the struggle and doubts and to find himself, at the age of 90, at the apex of a great and heroic lifetime.

Section One, "Lieber Meister," presents the first publication ever to be made of the letters between Frank Lloyd Wright and Louis H. Sullivan. The five years represented by these letters, 1918 to 1923, were difficult ones for both correspondents. Louis Sullivan had separated himself from the firm of Adler and Sullivan, and with that separation began a decline both in the amount and the quality of his work. Only occasional commissions, mostly insignificant, in the Midwest, were offered him. Frank Lloyd Wright was finishing his work on the Imperial Hotel in Japan, a commission which kept him out of the country for the better part of eight years. In the United States his work centered around several projects for Aline Barnsdall in Los Angeles, and the four world-famous concrete block houses—Millard, Storer, Freeman and Ennis—also in Los Angeles. The climax of those years of work was the devastating Kanto earthquake in

Tokyo in September of 1923, in which was conclusively proved the genius of his architecture-engineering by the way in which the Imperial Hotel withstood the ravages and destruction of the quake.

Section Two, "In the Cause of Architecture," traces his concern through letters addressed to both European and American architects that his work be understood as the cornerstone of an American Culture. In the early years of this century, while the United States looked persistently to Europe for eclectic styles in architecture, Frank Lloyd Wright was building an indigenous American architecture. Later, in the 1930's, he saw the influx of the International Style abnegating the principles of Organic Architecture. In these letters he is intense, eloquent and passionate in his wish that his nation subscribe to and develop a culture of its own.

In Section Three, "Letters to Critics," correspondence has been selected to include three specific persons: Henry-Russell Hitchcock, Lewis Mumford, and Howard Myers. These men offered Mr. Wright a special forum from which he could speak to the profession as a whole, most particularly through the medium of publication.

Section Four, "60 Years of Living Architecture," narrates, by means of letters to various architects concerned with the assembling and exhibition of the largest one man architectural exhibition ever to be produced, the details, trials, problems, and results of such a large undertaking. Although the problems were chiefly superficial, Mr. Wright took a keen and personal interest in the installation and exhibition of his work all the way from Philadelphia, where it opened, to Europe where it travelled extensively over a period of four years.

Section Five, "The R.I.B.A. and the A.I.A.," is more than just the recounting of the honors bestowed on Frank Lloyd Wright first in England, in 1941, and then in his own country, in 1949. It shows his concern for the profession of architecture in the moving address he gave at the occasion of his receiving the Gold Medal from the American Institute of Architects. He again and again reminds architects that their first loyalty must be to the art of architecture, not the profession of being architects. Concerning the role of the architect in society, he further wrote: "The artist-architect will be a man inspired by love of the nature of Nature, knowing that man is not made for architecture, architecture is made for man. He will see the practice of architecture never as a business but always religiously as basic to the welfare and culture of humanity as, at its best, it ever has been. And we must recognize the creative architect as poet and interpreter of life. We have only to consider what he has done and where he had been in every true culture of all time to see how important this son of culture is to our own future as a nation. This enrichment of life is the cause of Architecture, as I see it."

I

LIEBER MEISTER

The Great Fire that destroyed the major part of Chicago in 1871 made way for a wave of building construction that ushered in the beginning of a truly American architecture. That uniquely American creation—the skyscraper—was made feasible by construction methods and inventions such as the self-supporting metal frame and the elevator—which Frank Lloyd Wright defined as an "up-ended street." The tall building need no longer be a haphazard pile of stone or brick masonry stacked upon itself. Steel, glass, concrete and, finally, reinforced concrete—all the materials available and new technologies of the approaching twentieth century were now at hand. Nonetheless, the building technique for those structures rising in Chicago at the turn of the century was basically a "stick" architecture—the old post and beam construction that had typified carpentry buildings.

Into Chicago came many fine architects to take part in the needed rebuilding after the fire: Major William Le Baron Jenney, whose Home Insurance Building in Chicago (1883) was generally regarded as the first skyscraper, Daniel Burnham, John Wellborn Root, William Holabird, Martin Roche, Dankmar Adler and Louis Sullivan. Most of them worked at one time or another in the office of William Le Baron Jenney, and many of them had been trained as engineers. Therefore a great number of commercial buildings going up in Chicago from 1897 to 1900 were conceived from a structural rather than a decorative point of view. They were simple, strong of line, employed iron and steel skeleton construction, were as fireproof as a building could be in those days (the shadow of the Great Fire still lingered). They were sparse of ornament and employed much glass in a still prevailing post and beam construction. They were not plastered with the classical and renaissance entablatures and pediments that had pervaded architecture for the past five centuries. They were, in short, American, even Midwestern, to the utmost, their clean bold lines expressing commerce, industry, success.

Dankmar Adler was by far the most innovative of these Chicago architects. His knowledge of both architecture and structure had produced such perfect accoustics in his Central Music Hall that he was rightfully regarded as the foremost opera house designer of his time. Well established with a firm of his own, he soon realized his need for a design partner, and in 1879 he asked Louis Henri Sullivan to join him and found the firm of Adler and Sullivan.

Although the skyscraper as a practical solution to urban need for more space on constrained property was born here in Chicago, it took the genius of Louis Sullivan to create it not only as a functional innovation but as an aesthetic ideal.

In the Spring of 1887 young Frank Lloyd Wright ran away from his home in southwestern rural Wisconsin and came to the city of Chicago. As a boy of 18 he saw in Chicago on that rainy night when he arrived electric lights for the first time. It was to be an impression stamped strongly upon his memory for the rest of his life: brilliant, gleaming arcs of light made more dazzling by their reflection in the rain and mist. Intent on becoming an architect—his mother had determined that for him before he was born—he had studied engineering at the University of Wisconsin and had worked as a draftsman in the office of Alan Conover, the University engineer. But he felt constricted in his work at the University and he yearned to be part of a more active movement in architecture than Madison, Wisconsin could provide.

In Chicago he went first to work for architect J. Lyman Silsbee, but within a year he called upon Louis Sullivan. He applied for a job and was accepted.

Intuitively Frank Lloyd Wright grasped the nature of Louis Sullivan's genius, fathomed the quality of his work, was receptive to his ideas, and learned his technique of drawing and decoration. As Sullivan told him once, "Some day, Wright, people are not going to be able to tell who drew what, you or me." Sullivan installed him in a private office and gave him an assistant, George Elmslie. Only four offices were private in the firm of Adler and Sullivan in their new quarters in the Auditorium tower: those of Adler, Sullivan, Paul Mueller* (the foreman and builder for the firm) and Frank Lloyd Wright.

For nearly seven years Mr. Wright worked harmoniously with Louis Sullivan in the capacity of what he called "the pencil in his hand." But in 1893 a rupture occurred between them as a result of a private residence that Mr. Wright was building for an Adler-Sullivan client, Dr. Allison Harlan in Chicago. When Sullivan discovered that this work was going on, along with other commissions by Mr. Wright, he considered this to be a breach of contract and confronted him. Mr. Wright explained that he was doing this work on his own time, at home, not during office hours, in order to support his growing family. When he thus tried to justify this work, Sullivan fired him. That last meeting was heated and filled with temper and bitterness. Mr. Wright later wrote that, "I went home, my shame doubled. Although I often felt drawn to him in following years, I never went near him after that. It was nearly twenty years before I saw him again. This bad end to a glorious relationship has been a dark shadow to stay with me the days of my life."**

A depression hit America following the Columbian Exposition in 1893. The great building boom in Chicago was over, and no more work was coming to Adler and Sullivan. The Crane Company offered Adler $25,000 a year if he would sell Crane Elevators. Adler accepted and the firm was dissolved. Although many of their mutual friends and clients tried to encourage a reconciliation, it was hopeless. The work of neither of them, now independent of each other, would ever have the same dynamic impact or originality as their work done in collaboration.

When Mr. Wright came back to visit Dankmar Adler, now practicing by himself, still in Chicago, he "saw that something that had lived between the two men—who so needed each other always and even more so now—had already burned out. Again a world of high thought and fine feeling had come to a tragic end.

"We walked over from the Union League to the several small rooms the chief had taken on the Wabash Avenue side of the Auditorium, while his partner—now alone—was still carrying on up in the old offices of the tower. A heartbreaking situation. But I still believed they would come together.

*Mueller would later come to work for Mr. Wright on such famous structures as the Larkin Building, Unity Temple and the Imperial Hotel.

**from Frank Lloyd Wright, *Genius and the Mobocracy*, Duell, Sloan, and Pearce, 1949, New York.

"I said this when I left—feeling utterly futile. Worry and disappointment had already done something to the grand old chief. This was no way of life for him.

"In a short time he was dead."*

In 1918, a telephone call from Louis Sullivan to Mr. Wright at Taliesin, Wisconsin brought Mr. Wright down to Chicago to visit him. The friendship between the two that grew from this initial visit lasted the duration of Sullivan's life, and was one of unbroken affection and respect.

Sadness, tenderness, intimacy, and often desperation, permeate these letters between Frank Lloyd Wright and Louis Sullivan exchanged during the last five years of Sullivan's life as he was approaching his tragic end. He was beseiged by debts and poverty, forced to close his architectural office, frequently threatened eviction from the small, miserable hotel room which had become his home.

But the reconciliation between the two proved a great blessing to Sullivan. He now had someone upon whom he could lean for support, and the affection in these letters that flows between these two giants of architecture is deep and abiding. The "Wright" that Mr. Wright had always been to Mr. Sullivan before, in the days when he worked for him, had now become "Frank," and the "Mr. Sullivan," "Lieber Meister."

During the years of the span of letters between Mr. Wright and Mr. Sullivan, Mr. Wright was traveling back and forth across the Pacific for his work on the Imperial Hotel commission, in Tokyo. The design was made in 1914, construction continued well into 1922, eight intense and sometimes grueling years. He often found himself, despite the commission from the Hotel, with little or no money of his own. The expense of maintaining an architectural office in Tokyo, as well as in Los Angeles and frequently in Chicago, along with as his home and studio, Taliesin, in Wisconsin, was a financial drain on him. Added to these expenses was the unexpected cost of having to rebuild Taliesin after the tragic fire of 1914. But, whenever he could spare some money to help Louis Sullivan he gladly sent it.

*Ibid.

April 1, 1918
Frank Lloyd Wright
Taliesin, Spring Green, Wisconsin

Dear Frank:

Thank you for your affectionate letter which is most welcome. The cheque, too, indicates that you also are understanding.

I am not ill, Frank, and have not been recently. I simply have to "lay to," every once in a while, from sheer exhaustion due to too much corroding anxiety, and repair my strength as best I can. My worry is of course primarily a money worry, but it is truly awful to one of my nature. With the future blank I am surely living in hell. To think I should come to this at 61.

I understand you have much work and I am delighted accordingly. I see our friend Jens Jensen frequently. I have conceived an affection for this man and shall feel much alone when he moves to Ravinia [*Illinois*] May 1st.

I look forward to your coming at the end of the week. Let us not fail to connect. I have much to tell you that I cannot write. I am desperately in need of the right kind of companionship. No doubt you understand.

With full return of your affection believe me,

> Most sincerely,
> Louis H. Sullivan
> (Hotel Warner, Chicago. *All of the Sullivan correspondence in this section originates in Chicago.*)

I note that your letter is dated March 25th and was mailed March 27th. I read it only this morning. It may have been in the hotel office. Continue to address me at the hotel.

April 16, 1918
Frank Lloyd Wright
Taliesin, Spring Green, Wisconsin

Dear Frank:

The three volumes of "Jean Christophe" arrived at the hotel last evening. Thank you for sending them. I read the opening chapter this morning. It is charming: and the style so limpid and pure and simple. Of course it suffers in translation but I can feel the French of it nevertheless.

I am to lunch with John Heath tomorrow to further discuss matters. I wrote you recently concerning him and believe it highly desirable that you two should meet when you come to town—which I hope will be soon. I trust things are moving your way. I have much to discuss when we meet as I have been doing some tall thinking. I trust your mother is improving but Mr. Nagle has no word of her. Remember me kindly to Mrs. Noel [*Miriam Noel, Mr. Wright's second wife*].

                                   Sincerely,
                                   Louis H. Sullivan
                                   (the Cliff Dwellers)

May 18, 1918
Frank Lloyd Wright
Taliesin, Spring Green, Wisconsin

Dear Frank:

Am in an awful state of mind today. Have just received *peremptory* notice to pay this month's (current) office rent: $50.00. Mr. Geib of the Hotel Warner is also bringing some pressure. I told him you would be in town last Wednesday.

Now my dear Frank, I fancy you have troubles of your own and I hate to butt in, but I am terribly up in the air and want to find out where I am at if I can.

My efforts to raise money have been most disappointing. I wish I could have seen you to arrange if possible a modus vivendi. It seems an age since I saw you. Am trying to lighten cargo here but there is a lot of valuable stuff remaining. Wire me a night letter on receipt of this (if you get it Sunday). Better address it to the Cliff Dwellers, 220 South Michigan Ave., as I don't know what these people here may do. I hate to write in a panicky tone but I can't help it. It is hell!

> Sincerely,
> Sullivan
> (431 Wabash Avenue)

Please advise me at length.

Through Geo. Kimmon's suggestion I am working another line in Washington. One of his junior partners is a captain in the Construction division. I wrote to him Thursday. There is no opening in the P.O. Dept.

May 21, 1918
Frank Lloyd Wright
Taliesin, Spring Green, Wisconsin

Dear Frank:

Letter, enclosure and cheque rec'd. I return both thanks and sympathy. Thanks for the help extended and sympathy for the tension you are under. This morning found my office door locked against me: a childish procedure: followed by a demand for the *cash*. My plan is to raise the other half somehow, pay the rent and *get out* before the 1st and have the whole thing off my mind and yours.

Will write again very soon.

> Sincerely,
> Louis H. Sullivan
> (the Cliff Dwellers)

May 23, 1918
Frank Lloyd Wright
Taliesin, Spring Green, Wisconsin

Dear Frank:

I raised the balance of the money from Geo. Dean and have paid the May rent in full. (I was locked out a second time.) Am now working to get all my stuff out of here by the 1st of June.

An unexpected donation from Wm. Gates has enabled me to pay $20.00 on account at the hotel, and I can also pay up telephone bill and towel supply bill. Thus cleaning up the office score. All of this is a surprise, for the world looked blank to me Monday. I sincerely trust you will be able to dispose of some of your art work as I can keenly appreciate the strain you have been under. My especial regret is that I added to your burden. I am following two leads for a civilian gov't position: but so far no news. I am making my headquarters at the Cliffs [*Cliff Dwellers*] and have ordered my mail delivered there. But so far I have not determined how to store my stuff or where. I am feeling fine and for the time being have regained my elasticity.

I am enclosing a wire received from Junghandel [*Max Junghandel, a mutual acquaintance*]. Hope to see you here soon.

Sincerely,
Louis H. Sullivan
(431 Wabash Avenue)

May 24, 1918
Frank Lloyd Wright
Taliesin, Spring Green, Wisconsin

Dear Frank:

Am tired and stiff this evening. It's hard work getting my stuff winnowed and packed. Don't know yet where I shall store it.

Am enclosing Junghandel's letter of the 21st. Am writing him a line to the effect that he should "extend the same courtesy" to you.

News received from Washington is not encouraging, but I must keep on trying.

Hope to see you here soon.

Sincerely,
Louis H. Sullivan
(the Cliff Dwellers)

June 1, 1918
Frank Lloyd Wright
Taliesin, Spring Green, Wisconsin

Dear Frank:

My stuff went to warehouse yesterday and I turned over my office key. This gives me a sense of relief—and I am foot-loose and ready to jump at whatever my offer: U.S. East—California—Japan—Timbuctoo—anywhere. My health is excellent and I am not "downhearted" yet. I have however no encouraging news from Washington.

Yesterday I received a very, very warmhearted personal letter from Max Junghandel. To which I have replied. It seems to me it would be a fine thing to put through the Japanese deal with him. I am enclosing copy of this letter to Chatham (May 28). I have warned him (M. J.) to keep away from the packing house gang. I know their methods. Hope to see you here soon and am anxious to meet Mitchell Kennerly. Take time to drop me a line as to when you will be here so we can canvass the entire situation.

Sincerely,
Louis H. Sullivan
(the Cliff Dwellers)

June 10, 1918
Frank Lloyd Wright
Taliesin, Spring Green, Wisconsin

Dear Frank:

Called up Hadel today who said you were personally much occupied—working day and night—and that he did not know if you would be in town this week. I hope he is mistaken as to the latter statement.

I don't get much encouragement from Washington, though I have a pleasant letter from Max Dunning [a fellow architect] giving some hope. Meanwhile, very naturally I am doing considerable "aviation" work. I get a personal letter occasionally from Max Junghandel. In his latest—rec'd today—he seems to have a vague idea that I perhaps might go to Japan. This puts a little bee in my bonnet, and my first impulse is, very naturally, to ask you if any tangible basis could be found for such an idea. Not having any notion as to what your plans may be I can only trust that the query is not indiscreet.

I must find some basis of activity or I will be on my uppers for fair. By the way, can you give me any further information as to Mitchell Kennerly? Claude Bragdon has written me stating that he would like to undertake to boost the publication of my "Kindergarten Chats." I have told him to go ahead if he feels confident he can put it through. I am now going over the ms. to see if it needs revision. I have not found much to change so far. It's good stuff today and I should like to see it in book form. I have asked Bragdon to write to you on the subject.

I should like to have a good chat with you as soon as may be over matters in general and in particular. For I value your judgment. You have a much shrewder sense than I. Drop me a line if you can—if only a few words. Am very well.

Sincerely,
Louis H. Sullivan
(the Cliff Dwellers)

July 25, 1918
Frank Lloyd Wright
Taliesin, Spring Green, Wisconsin

Dear Frank:

Sorry to have missed you yesterday. I assume you had no time to spare. I would like to know what is the "good news" you mentioned in your meteoric flight.

Am having a skirmish with Knopf the publisher over the K.C.s [Kindergarten Chats]. Have forwarded his letter together with a copy of my reply to Bragdon. Have a pretty bad case of summer months cold today. Otherwise am as happy as circumstances permit: and they don't permit. Which reminds me of the squib, "So and So is nothing if not accurate, and he is not accurate."

Hope you can squeeze out a minute to drop me a line. Have not heard from Junghandel in quite a while. Fancy he must be getting discouraged.

As ever,
Louis H. Sullivan
(the Cliff Dwellers)

November 4, 1918
Frank Lloyd Wright
Imperial Hotel, Tokyo

Dear Frank:

Your letter, mailed at sea, reached me this morning. To find a cheque in it positively paralyzed me, for I was at the very end of my string: and I had assumed that you would need your resources in full for the trip. It came therefore all the more welcome because it came as a complete surprise. But I was much pleased anyway. I feared you might have no time for correspondence until you reached Japan, because you made such a flying trip through Chicago.

Yesterday (I should say Saturday) I rec'd a visit from your young Japanese friends Fujikura and Endo. The latter impressed me as particularly intelligent. They proposed leaving immediately for Washington to facilitate obtaining passports and expected to return here in two weeks or so. I presume you will get all the war news by wireless, but the latest today is that Austria has signed an armistice and that Turkey has opened up the Dardanelles and the Bosphorus to the Allied fleet. This will of course be stale news when it reaches you, as I suppose you will not receive this letter in less than a month or six weeks.

As to the Kindergarten Chats, I completed the manuscript on Oct. 6th. Since then it has been in the hands of Geo. Dean's stenographer, who is giving what time she can spare to the work. She is very accurate, her errors being almost entirely typographical. I have thus far proof-read 15 chapters (out of the 52).

This week has been a godsend to me inasmuch as it gave me serious mental occupation.

My banker friends in Manistique are slow (as all country bankers are) but their letters seem to indicate actual business very soon.

You can imagine the difficulty of raising (or rather trying to raise) money after the strain of the 4th Liberty Loan. Still, my friends have stood by me pretty well, and I can't blame them if they are getting a little poorer everyday. I hope you will write me soon after this, and I will try to keep you posted on the news here.

Hope you will succeed in connecting up with Junghandel—he seems the right man to me. Thank you for your warm expressions of affection which are wholeheartedly reciprocated.

Sincerely,
Louis H. Sullivan
(the Cliff Dwellers)

December 19, 1918
Frank Lloyd Wright
Imperial Hotel, Tokyo

Dear Frank:

I trust you have arrived safely and that all is well. I have a few items of news: first, an utter pandemonium here on the 6th and the 11th of Nov. It was astounding. Someone called it a "peace riot." Next: my portrait 3/4 length has been painted by Frank Werner. It is a fine work: and most important of all my book has been type-written, corrected and bound: and a copy forwarded to Claude Bragdon a few days since. It is now up to him and the publisher. I feel much relaxed after so strenuous and long-continued an effort, and at present have no focus. I have escaped the "flu" but have had colds and muscular stiffness, quite annoying. There is a shout for some business, a bank in northern Michigan. It is moving very...[*The conclusion of this letter is missing*]

January 20, 1919
Frank Lloyd Wright
Imperial Hotel, Japan

Dear Frank:

I had hoped to hear from you by this time, but presume you have your hands full in Nippon. Anyway I trust everything is going well with you.

10 days ago I was given a bank remodeling job at Manistique, Mich. It doesn't run heavily into money, but will keep the wolf away for a couple of months.

Today I rec'd a letter from Max Junghandel telling me that you and he had connected finally on the Tokyo project, and [he] has asked me to assist him in obtaining a permit to leave the country, by writing favorably to a certain office in Washington. This I will gladly do and will forward M. J. tomorrow a first draft of such letter for his approval or correction. I suppose Schindler [*Architect Rudolph M. Schindler was in charge of Mr. Wright's Los Angeles building projects during his stay in Japan*] keeps you posted on local news. There are some signs of revival and we may come to an even keel in time.

I escaped the "flu" and am feeling very fit. I have found this club a great comfort. I finished the book [*Kindergarten Chats*] but there are publication troubles, so that I am uncertain as to when the work will appear. However I can wait six months or a year until publishers get over being crazy, as they certainly now are.

Affectionately,
Louis H. Sullivan
(the Cliff Dwellers)

April 10, 1919
Louis H. Sullivan
Chicago, Illinois

My dear Meister Sullivan,

Both your letters have reached me here with their touch of news and good cheer.

I am glad of the completion of the book and the new work. Both are tonic in effect—I am sure.

A clipping from the Tribune came a day or two ago, illustrations of Werner's portrait and the charge of pro-Germanism discussed. It seems a fine work and a likeness. Also the magazine used Tallmadge's article. His appreciation is shallow enough.

I have written no letters since I have been here to anyone, except the business ones necessary to the office and a few to my mother.

It has often been on my mind to write to you however—but I have been much occupied—nearly every moment. When not engaged in preparation for building, all Japan seems hunting me up with enticing "Nishikiye" [*color prints*] which are a pursuit in themselves, absorbing and financially devastating.

I have spent every cent I could collect or borrow or overdraw on them in a final grand attempt to pay my debts out of existence on my return in July.

My previous work here and the enormous sums expended in my own and in behalf of others has made me the shining mark among those who have the "charming things" in their possession.

I have had remarkable success this time with two old families—securing treasures the dealers never set their fakey old eyes on before.

I shall make a commotion in the print world when I return—and hope to do so to my financial advantage in cold blood and in perfect form.

You might help me at the Cliff Dwellers by dropping the hint to Shaw and others that I have a collection made in the past six months that Monsieur Vevet himself would envy! An exhibition at the Art Institute in September or October might be arranged—for the finest things of the kind in the world? Then I might send them on to New York and sell them there. Meantime I am broke but as I have my living here and transportation home I am sure to arrive in fairly well-fed condition.

You will find it difficult to believe, but I have succeeded in putting into this thing more than 170,000.00 yen or over $85,000.00. That is quite a sum and scares me when I think of it. My eggs are all in one basket.

The Hotel people here have helped me by advancing my entire commission so I might speculate with it and double it—as the work drags here frightfully and I am going to lose any compensation I might have had for my own time.

The Government here is slow and eternal. There was a young fellow at the Imperial Hotel here (left a week or two ago) who came to take delivery to the Government on 125 motor trucks. He came in November, early. The trucks were unloaded on the wharf at Yokohama, assigned to the Government, but the Government had no money to pay the duty of 35% upon them to the Government. Itself had no money to pay itself. So the young fellow waited five months and so did the trucks on the wharf until the appropriation was passed in late March and the duty paid in April. That is how things move here. We have our bricks on the ground, our stone out, our force collecting ready to strike, and some Government buildings still are in our way on the site. The Government has no authority to sell them, no money to move them. There they are. I guess we shall have to build them in and let the Government pick them out like a decayed kernel from a nut, when they can.

I have had a chance to build two more fine hotels here on fine sites in other cities, but when the contracts were about to be signed the matter came to the attention of the directors of the Imperial Hotel at their board meeting and Baron Okura objected, sustained by Baron Shibusawa, backed up heartily by Murai San and Asano San, two of the richest men and most powerful in Japan. They didn't want their "imported" architect shared by others until their job was finished.

I said, all right—if they wanted to buy me out I didn't mind, but they would have to keep me busy themselves with new projects as I couldn't thrive on the one they had given me.

They agreed that something should be done and said they would do something. Whereupon I canceled my contract in one case and declined to sign in another. But they have done nothing extra yet. However it gives me a claim upon them in a way which they may hear from later. Maybe they will keep their promise.

Many hotels are needed here and many beautiful sites available.

They didn't object to anything but hotels, I understand—but I think they are keeping prospective clients away from me as much as they can.

This is still a Feudal Isle in many respects. We are very comfortable here—two rooms and bath in a sunny angle of the hotel. An office, good drafting room fitted out in a wooden building on the new site.

I fixed up with Max Junghandel to be here in February, but he is still nailed down in San Francisco—German descent! Can you do anything? We have sent him money and he has it about spent and wants, or will soon, more. But it is up to him to get here—morally responsible for his appearance here—and I do not like my position on his behalf, in its present state, at all. Can you do anything for him?

Do continue to drop me an occasional line. I am always anxious to learn news of you and my neglect of your notes until now is significant only of my procrastinating preoccupation—a sign of selfishness too I must admit—without feeling that the admission gets me anything I ought to have.

Affectionately as always yours,
Frank

I wanted to put a check in this letter as I fear you may be needing it in spite of your cheerful letters, but I can't now—it reposes along with other prospective pleasures and pressing obligations in the profound heart of the Nishikiye!

Something will come out of it in time. When I am strong [*enough*] to lay my own enemies in the dust yours won't go unscathed!

December 25, 1919
Frank Lloyd Wright
Imperial Hotel, Tokyo

Dear Frank:

I had a most delightful shock of surprise on the 23d when I rec'd a Xmas note from Schindler with an enclosure. I was not in the least looking for anything of the sort, but it enabled me to do some things for others and for myself that otherwise I could not have done. It was certainly a token of affection on your part which I shall ever cherish.

Thuswise on this day I convey to you the heartfelt greeting which the season implies. May you have health, long life, happiness and that prosperity which is your due.

I hope the journey o'er land and sea was not too uncomfortable and that Madame Noel did not suffer too much. Convey to her my kind remembrances and warmest greetings. May she be happy also.

There is some news to relate: I was invited to visit St. John's Military Academy at Delafield, Wis. (near Oconomowoc) and made such visit. It seems they are proposing to raise $125,000.00 for a memorial chapel to be dedicated to those of its alumni and students (some 500 in number—fifty of whom were slain—for Wall St.) who were in service. They wish me to handle the work and prepare a sketch to help in the propaganda. Strange to say they actually wish to pay for this preliminary. You may know or know of Dr. Smythe, the President. He is an Episcopal clergyman of rather open-minded and considerable culture. It seems that the commandant of cadets, Major Farrana, was in Owatonna, Minn., and saw my bank there. It impressed him, if you please, as having an ecclesiastical character: and I am wondering if there is any basis for that impression. The school enrollment is 500 and they do not wish to expand. (Sensible idea in these days of quantity production and inferior output.) However they wish 1,000 sittings, which won't do for the money. When I get this item reduced and several others settled in my mind, will form an idea, but not until then.

My library project at DeKalb, Ill. is still dragging. It is all settled that I am to do the work, but they have not yet been able to raise the funds necessary to cover my services.

I am now getting matters in shape at Columbus, Wis. (my bank). It was an awful mess to straighten out. Other bank "prospects" I am letting rest until conditions become more settled.

You will regret to learn that Geo. Dean died Dec. 10th of pneumonia after a three days' illness. It was a severe shock to me; for with all his little weaknesses Geo. was a staunch friend to me and proved it in 1918 by helping to pull me through that nightmare year.

I don't know of any other news except that for the first time in years I am having a pleasant Xmas.

I want to read over again my manuscript "Democracy" and will then forward it to you. I am curious to see what impression it will make on me, as I have not looked into it for years.

Schindler wrote to the Roy Crofters. They say they would like to look into the matter. He will forward the ms. Let us see what happens.

I shall miss you very much. Do make a special effort and write once in a while.

> Affectionately,
> Louis H. Sullivan
> (Hotel Warner)

April 4, 1920
Frank Lloyd Wright
Imperial Hotel, Tokyo

Dear Frank:

This is Easter Sunday: a northeast blizzard is raging and the lake is in an uproar. Christ is arisen! But he will set with the day's hour and be gone for another year. Let us be thankful the pretense lasts but a day—tomorrow we return to normal.

We had quite a scare—some of us—regarding your illness—cablegram from you; your mother departing hurriedly with a physican, etc. Finally I was inspired to phone your son David, and was reassured—you were convalescent. Since then I have wished to write you, but day by day has passed. I have been too beastly tired at night and too preoccupied by day.

Have been at work on a hurry up bank remodeling job at Manistique, Mich.—a good plan, but a potboiler otherwise. Draftsmen not to be had. Finally after a month's self-work, broken back, weary legs, frazzled nerves, I got Campbell to let me have two sophomore boys from Armour. They have done surprisingly well, which shows they have not been spoiled, *as yet.* Or perhaps Campbell has a little sense. The boys relieved me of drudgery (pleasant novelty for them no doubt, but hell for me)....[*the conclusion of this letter is missing*]

August 6, 1920
Louis H. Sullivan
The Cliff Dwellers, Chicago

Lieber Meister,

This will introduce Mr. Kawamoto, a young Japanese architect whose footsteps are directed toward the fountain head of architectural wisdom by this little note of introduction.

I think of you often with affection and respect and would like a walk and a talk with you—which I hope I may have—soon.

I am quite well again—"hoping you are the same—"

Frank

Kawamoto San is in the employ of the Mitsui, the powerful capitalistic clan of Japan—he is going to New York to study architecture with the Fuller Company. He strays from his path, you see—

November 30, 1920
Frank Lloyd Wright
Los Angeles, California

Dear Frank:

Sorry I won't be able to see you before you leave for Japan, but my blessings will go with you anyway. Drop me a line, if you can, before sailing.

Please tell Schindler I rec'd his note and am very sorry to have missed connection with him as he passed through Chicago.

However I will await with interest his promised letter. Trust everything is going well with you. Have thought very often of you. There is some prospect of work in the spring. At present all I am doing is the pedestal for Leonard Crunelli's statue of Gov. Palmer to be placed in Springfield. Am in pretty good health and exercising as much patience as I can.

Affectionately,
Louis H. Sullivan
(the Cliff Dwellers)

August 19, 1921
Frank Lloyd Wright
Imperial Hotel, Tokyo

Dear Frank:

I have just cabled you as follows: "Am in trouble. What can you do in the shortest time."

I had not expected, when you were here, to be forced to send such a message, and the explanation is delays, delays, delays, with continuing expenses until I will be on the rocks (real rocks) in about 10 days. I don't suppose you care about details—they are tiresome. The main point is that I have been hung up by the thumbs for weeks and the nervous strain has become unbearable—hence this cable, and my hope that you will be able to respond.

In view of the miscarriage of the letter you mailed me last December it may be proper to say here that in case you wrote me from the Coast, before leaving, no such letter has reached me to date. What I have learned about the Japanese mail service (on inquiry at the P.O. here) is rather disheartening. I fancy that you are already in Tokyo—and that this letter will reach you some time under 30 days. Hence the urgency of my cable.

I trust you had a pleasant trip and that all is well with the work and with yourself.

It is a constant regret with me that we had so little time together here: for there are few people I like or respect sufficiently to care about their personal doings, or esteem enough to take it for granted they have any real object in life; and this in spite of the fact that there are many well-meaning men who call themselves friends and who doubtless are such, as they see things.

Well, this is the jumping off place.

Affectionately,
Louis H. Sullivan
(the Cliff Dwellers)

August 23, 1921
Frank Lloyd Wright
Imperial Hotel, Tokyo

Dear Frank:

If you have any money to spare, now is the urgent time to let me have some. As I do not know how you are fixed, I cannot specify any sum; I can merely say that I am in a very serious situation: indeed it is now a sheer matter of food and shelter.

So many of my friends are out of town on vacations that the situation has become very peculiar—I seem to have lost my way.

There are two rifts in the overhanging clouds of the general situation: two encouraging letters from bankers, one from Iowa and one from Georgia. These with several other good prospects should make me busy when the tide turns. Meanwhile the immediate problem is to keep on earth. These letters were very recently rec'd.

With kindest,
Louis H. Sullivan
(1808 Prairie Avenue)

November 30, 1922
Louis H. Sullivan
1808 Prairie Avenue, Chicago

Lieber Meister,

I am going to tell you a secret, which I hope you will keep—I am extremely hard up, and not a job in sight in the world. My "selling" campaigns have failed. I am anxious about you always and hope all is well with you—at least enough so that the "vie d'interieur" is undisturbed. If things get desperately bad and you are in a serious way you must know that I would share my last crust with you, and I hope you will always let me know whenever that time threatens.

I enclose something of what I have left, to insure you something of Christmas as by that time I may be far away on the quest for work.

Affectionately,
Frank

February 5, 1923
Louis H. Sullivan
The Cliff Dwellers, Chicago

Lieber Meister,

Breakfast is ready!
Sorry to come away without seeing you.
Have pitched in here to locate.
Perhaps you will come out later—to see this ice cream, cake, and soda water corner of the world.

Affectionately,
Frank
(Los Angeles)

March 3, 1923
Louis H. Sullivan
The Cliff Dwellers, Chicago

Lieber Meister,

No word comes from you and I am wondering if you are perhaps ill. The weather here is remarkably fine—round clear sun—I have rented a house for a studio and am at work.

Mrs. Barnsdall (of Olive Hill) has given me a new home to build for her at Beverly—in a beautiful 12 acre mountainside.

Mrs. Millard of Highland Park has given me another little studio house on a charming lot—these with Mr. Moore makes three "repeaters" in the office at the same time. Three clients who "came back."

What about the [Architectural] Record article? I see by a prospectus just handed me that February and March numbers are full—in which case unless something definite is decided upon by Mikkelsen at once I must look elsewhere, because something must happen [for me] to go back to Japan.

Will you kindly search Andy to see what he really knows about the matter? And let me know and let me know about yourself—did you receive my enclosure?

Affectionately,
Frank
(Los Angeles)

April 2, 1923
Louis H. Sullivan
The Cliff Dwellers, Chicago

Lieber Meister,

I have asked Mr. Horton to have you go over the galley proofs of my article to save a week's time or more and also to avail myself of your superior abilities in this respect. Censor anything you want to. I have rearranged the first draft sent to Horton to eliminate repetition and get the divisional headings more into place. This, I dare say will reach him before he has the text set up.

Won't you give him some help in way of advice if he needs it in make-up.

I have sent you three revised articles if you care to peruse them, one of which, "The Modifying Member," is the answer to Mullgardt to be printed in May number of the same magazine in which his fancy work appeared.

(The second, "The best, I think," is not yet placed in Propaganda I.)

The third, "The Third Dimension," is written for Wendingen—to go out with the number they are getting out devoted to my work.

I also send a copy of a letter received from Editor Fleisher apropos of the Hotel and the article Mullgardt got printed in his paper in Tokyo.

Thinking to do me a favor he eliminated from my article "He Who Gets Slapped" all the poison and printed merely the sob stuff and self justification. Ye Gods! Our friends! It makes me sick. You wouldn't have known me—that apologetic, tame, miserable reply that came out from his editorial shears!

He meant well, I am sure, but poor consolation. His letter though is welcome.

Write me how you are—and what news? A nice note from Jens. What a loveable soul is his—and a nice word of appreciation from Carl Sandburg. Apropos of one from me concerning the Rootabaga Stories. Man alive! there is poetry! I love these little indigenous poems.

Nothing big here yet—but maybe soon. I long for the substantial background of old Chicago. This is all "to be." The region has been cruelly "exploited"—and is so still. I don't know if they want anything in the way of the third dimension [organic architecture] yet. We'll see.

Affectionately,
Frank

Won't you take the trouble to get the two articles I labored with in vain while in Chicago from Max Dunning, together with the photographs I sent to him with them.

The idea was, at that time, to take this treacherous attack before the Institute—but what's the use? The further I get from it, the more I believe myself an ass to have got into such a rage with a futile worm like the author of it. He did a lot of harm at the time and I was helpless. He timed it so well for a damned cheap purpose.

June 8, 1923
Louis H. Sullivan
The Cliff Dwellers, Chicago

Lieber Meister,

I have not written since the fragrance of your "bouquet" reached me in print. Very well done by Mikkelsen, who kindly distributed fifty or more copies for me at home and abroad.

My friends think it a fine dignified piece of writing and an evidence of a noble spirit on your part—and an act in itself unique. I am sure the effect of it will be good for us both and for THE CAUSE to which we have both given our lives.

I hope all is well with you. I miss you very much. Frankly I am homesick. Will return [*from Los Angeles*] for the autumn months to Taliesin and we will see something of each other there, I hope.

As a birthday present (my birthday) I enclose a feeble insufficient practical matter—intended to dispel tiresome visions and ward off evil spirits for the moment.

What of the Autobiography? Most autobiographies are a form of auto-intoxication—something like getting a man crying drunk in order to get him to tell you all he knows. If he really knows something, as you do, the result is invariably profitable, as it probably is always interesting if the man himself is so.

I hope your pencil is not idle on account of your pen.

Affectionately,
Frank

Frank Lloyd Wright, 1887

Dankmar Adler

Louis H. Sullivan

Louis H. Sullivan: the Wainwright Building

Frank Lloyd Wright, 1893

Winslow House

Ennis House

Imperial Hotel, Tokyo

Imperial Hotel, Tokyo

Frank Lloyd Wright, 1924

August 28, 1923
Louis H. Sullivan
The Cliff Dwellers, Chicago

Lieber Meister,

When I learned from you of the death of your little companion [a *milliner who used to visit him*]—I was too unhappy to make you unhappier by writing anything at all. I know by experience that only silence is best at such times—no words touch the ache except to increase it. But a longer time has gone by than I intended owing to pressure of affairs here and a natural procrastination—

You are, I see from your account of your work, on an even keel again—but of course you must be frightfully lonely in the needs the little companion met—

I am not going to Europe but I am coming home in October to see you—if for nothing else. Taliesin needs some attention. My affairs here are still in the bud—*promising* that is all. [*The next few lines are illegible.*]

I hope you can join me here for the winters—they are too severe in Chicago—I may be able to arrange it if any good comes to me here—here's hoping.

> Affectionately,
> Frank
> (Los Angeles)

The remaining correspondence with Louis Sullivan revolves around the survival of the Imperial Hotel, which officially opened in Tokyo on July 4, 1922. In constructing it Mr. Wright had employed a number of ingenious methods to ward off the effects of Tokyo's all too frequent earthquakes and the fires that accompanied them. His letter dated September 26, 1923 (see below) describes those methods, which had been opposed by Japanese financiers and deprecated by many of his colleagues.

On September 1, 1923 Tokyo experienced the worst earthquake in its history. It killed some 140,000 people and left the city a burning shambles—except for the Imperial Hotel! This first-hand account from architect Arata Endo, Mr. Wright's Japanese associate, recaptures the moment and explains the excitement in the letters that follow. [Ed. note: I have taken the liberty of making Mr. Endo's letter adhere more closely to

American English idiom; the essential contents, however, remain the same as in the original.]

September 8, 1923
Frank Lloyd Wright
Los Angeles, California, U.S.A.

Lieber Meister,

What a glory it is to see the Imperial standing amidst the ashes of the whole city!

First came the shock, without any previous signs of any kind. I rushed out of the house and ran to the Imperial Grille Court at the rear of the building. Posts of the porte-cochere there were cracked, the ground was cracked and rolling just like waves, and water sprang up along the crevices. I couldn't hold myself upright, and the building shook just like a little toy or something, the victory statue on top dancing and quivering perilously. Down came the restaurant in the park across the street, and fire broke out the next moment. Taisho Kaku, the restaurant across on the other street, had its roof flat on the ground.

Horror stricken people kept running to and fro, the women weeping like children, etc., etc. These were the sights on the street as I stood at the front of the hotel right after the shock ceased. Four stone figures fell, two of them into the pool where they sank out of sight as if they had never existed.

There was no damage in the front lobby, the perforated lanterns on those four big pillars as tranquil as ever. There was no damage in the dining room, except that a temporary partition had fallen. The corner piers of the dining room showed some cracks, but none of them serious. The Theatre was intact and the upper story banquet hall was as glorious as ever. Just when I got up there, some 40 feet above the ground, slam-bang came a second quake with a horrible roar. I was swept off my feet. Staggering and dizzy I got to a pillar and held on. From there I saw the private dining room to the south showing absolutely no sign of the effects of the shock.

So the Imperial has come through the test and she stands like the sun. Glory to you, Lieber Meister.

The Metropolitan Police Building and others, those three story brick buildings, survived the quakes but were destroyed by fire. The Imperial

Theatre suffered the same fate. The Fuller Building, next to the Theatre, was seriously destroyed, its steel framework bent like iron tongs. The Nagai Building, in the process of construction, was shattered to pieces and hundreds of workmen were crushed underneath. All steel buildings proved fatal, enough to show that our architects were fools.

The first shock was enough to lay many buildings flat, and on top of that came a second, just as strong, within five minutes. This second shock easily leveled what the first had loosened. And those that somehow survived the second shock were not safe either, because of the fires that followed. They say fires were seen started in 26 places around the city, helped by strong winds.

As regards private homes, the old style "go-downs" were seriously damaged. Those traditional mud houses proved utterly inefficient against earthquakes of this magnitude. Tiles were moved like sheets, walls peeled off, the houses' contents naked, open to destruction by whatever rains or fires followed—not an exception to this in the entire city.

Korean rioters and socialists also worked together in setting fires to the remains of important buildings during the night.

Fire billowed from every house, and those people who survived the crush and sought places of safety out in the open were killed by the smoke and scorching hot air, roasted by hundreds and thousands.

One of my relatives is known to have been snatched from his boat in the Sumida River—the safest refuge you can imagine—and dashed into the waters. Fire hemmed in the crowd at both ends of the Ryogoku Bridge, and then the bridge caught fire and down it went. So forth and so forth—more than anyone can possibly describe.

Hayashi San, at the Imperial, is overjoyed; his family is there and is safe.

Now your chance is here. You will be received here now with admiration and appreciation—late, yes, but not too late. The whole city is at your disposal. Your work here has been prepared for you. You will have more appreciation now than in America. Therefore you had best come here where it is more worthwhile to plant your footsteps than in Los Angeles—don't you think?

With this hope and ever increasing love,

Arata Endo

September 3, 1923
Frank Lloyd Wright
Los Angeles, California

Dear Frank:

I am greatly agitated over the news from Tokyo. The calamity is terrible to think of. I am especially anxious for definite news as to the "Imperial"—as of course you are.

If that went, I don't see how anything else can remain standing. The
whole affair is shocking, the loss of life especially. When you get authentic news let me know. I don't trust the newspaper reports in detail thus
far.

This is my birthday: 67 long years of experience, which after all may
amount to little. I am beginning to feel that I have received a mortal
wound, although perhaps it is too early to say. We shall see. Never
before have I felt how sordid are the faces one sees upon the street. The
glow of an inner nature is so rare as to be startling and disconcerting to a
degree.

I would like very much to get away for the winter, but as yet I see no
way to manage it. Just now I am awaiting word from Macon, Ga. to see if
the bank project there is to materialize immediately. I am in very fair
health now, but dread the pull of the winter. I had a pretty bad time with
the "flu" last February which disabled me for two months; and a possible
repetition has become something of a nightmare with me.

As I look out the window at the lake, the view is amazingly serene.
We have only a handful at dinner nowadays, but the numbers will increase very soon.

Affectionately,
Louis Sullivan
(the Cliff Dwellers)

SEPTEMBER 8, 1923
LOUIS H. SULLIVAN
CLIFF DWELLERS, CHICAGO

DIRECT WIRE FROM TOKYO. PURPOSELY SECURED BY HARRY
CHANDLER, EDITOR OF THE LOS ANGELES TIMES. REPORTS IMPERIAL
HOTEL UNDAMAGED, MENTIONING ONLY SIX OTHER BUILDINGS AS

STANDING IN TOKYO, BUT DAMAGED. YANKEE SKYSCRAPERS NOW
ONLY TWISTED SKELETONS WITH NOTHING ON THEIR BONES. CHEER
UP, LEIBER MEISTER, OUR FORTUNE IS MADE. NOTIFY OLIVER GALE
AND OTHERS. WILL SEE YOU SOON.

                                        FRANK

September 24, 1923
Louis H. Sullivan
The Cliff Dwellers, Chicago

Lieber Meister,

This is "official" at last and there are no words—it is stupendous.
Another wire this morning from Hayashi (former manager) and Endo San,
my Japanese right bower says: "Imperial stands square and
straight—congratulations." Will see you in two weeks about. This ought
to have publicity but upon my word, I don't know how to go about it.
Perhaps you know someone.

                                        Hastily,
                                        Frank
                                        (Los Angeles)

Will you see that Oliver Gale, Jens Jensen, and Howard Shaw see the
cablegram?

September 26, 1923
Louis H. Sullivan
The Cliff Dwellers, Chicago

Lieber Meister,

Your letter regarding the telegram came.
I forgot to say that Okura is the name of the Baron who is president of
the company owning and operating the hotel. IMPEHO is the cable word
officially denoting that company—contracted you see from Imperial
Hotel.

The wire was sent to Spring Green as Okura does not know that I am in Los Angeles.

I have received another cable from Tokyo reading "Imperial stands square and straight." signed Hayashi, who was the manager that came to America to get me, and signed Endo, who was my Japanese right bower in my office in Tokyo.

Corroboration comes now from every side.

The Yankee skyscrapers are some of them standing, badly wracked and some with the top floors shaken down—all visibly seriously damaged, probably murdering thousands trapped in them—unable to get out.

Several are completely gutted by fire also.

Of course it is impossible to tell how the strain has really affected the connections still hidden by whatever of "architecture" is left clinging to their bones.

People die of panic and fright and elevators don't run in an earthquake. You can imagine the piles of dead on the stair landings—stairs four feet wide—10 stories high—half-flights.

And this congestion on the basis of eight or ten stories, where it was already too great for safety or comfort on the basis of three stories, was a crime, but a tribute to Yankee salesmanship. I am opposed to the tall buildings from now on, in the Pacific Basin, even if the human scale of things and safety and convenience are to be sacrificed to the ubiquitous American Landlord. I have written something outlining these views which will appear somewhere perhaps, and I am sending it to Tokyo to try and head off the propaganda which will try to rebuild Tokyo as a modern American city.

You might join me if you think I am right. I'll send a copy of the article.

What saved the Imperial was the principle of flexibility: flexible foundations, flexible connections, flexible piping and wiring systems, flexible continuous slabs cantilevering over supports, passing clear through the outer walls to become balconies or projecting cornices—and an exaggeration of all vertical supporting members, center of gravity always kept low as possible.

My scheme for the construction of the central roofing—central high group—about the equivalent of a seven story building, I think particularly sound in this respect and will show it to you in detail when I arrive, which I hope will be in about a week from now.

The cantilever which looked both dangerous and absurd to the critics absolutely trimmed and balanced the structure in the undulations, upheavals and twists. It is officially reported by an eyewitness that no person was even injured in any way in the Imperial Hotel. So the anxiety concerning the stone or lava forms which faced the concrete was ill considered also. Lead piping only was all I permitted in the structure, joints wiped, all kept free of the construction. A pipe shaft looked like a section of one's abdomen—just "guts."

The pipes swept with bends from the trenches into the shafts and from the shafts to the bathroom fixtures. The only screwed joints I permitted in the structure were those at the fixtures in the nickel fittings of the bathrooms.

Flexibility and lightness, overhead, and everything free of the structure in the way of service systems—no iron piping—monolithic construction divided at proper intervals clear through the building (the Imperial is thus vertically cut into about twelve sections) and through transverse reinforcing in all lateral members, hooking into or onto the vertical reinforcement: these are the principles on which the Imperial was, with great personal devotion, built.

Mueller's untiring attention to the execution of the details of this program counted too in the final result. Nothing of any importance was put into place without his superintendence.

I wonder where the old boy is? He will be delighted, for he was not all together sure I was right about my foundation or about a number of other things.

Anyhow the cataclysm has marked the end of the controversy. The Journals here on the coast have been liberal in Editorials, Cartoons and leading articles, but it is surprising how little is accomplished without continuous follow-up publicity.

This publicity I need and want, to strengthen my arm in the coming tussle with what Starrett stands for in toto and in Tokyo.

Help me all you can, I know you will.

You are the best good sport I know. I am looking forward to a reunion—and breakfast will be ready as usual at the Congress.

What a different sense of our situations will be present at this time.

Last time I was in a smothered rage that knocked my sentiments into a heap in which I could find no good order.

Here's to you—and hoping,

Affectionately,
Frank
(Los Angeles)

Louis Sullivan died less than seven months after this letter was written. But before his death he placed in Mr. Wright's hands a sheaf of more than 122 of his original sketches and drawings, saying to him: "Some day, Frank, you will be writing about these." Mr. Wright promised that he would indeed do so, and in 1949 he wrote and published the book Genius and the Mobocracy, a moving account of his work with Louis Sullivan and a vivid explanation of the genius of his Lieber Meister.

On April 11, 1924, Frank Lloyd Wright visited him for the last time. They discussed Mr. Sullivan's newly published Autobiography and the state of architecture in general. "It is you who has created the new architecture in America," Sullivan acknowledged, "but I do not believe you could have done it without me." Three days later Sullivan was dead.

During his next three decades of inexhaustible creativity, Mr. Wright never forgot his ties with Louis Sullivan, as the following letters reveal.

July 7, 1953
Mr. Frank Lloyd Wright
Taliesin, Spring Green, Wisconsin

My dear Frank,

Recently I have undertaken to write an opus on the influence of the World Columbian Exposition, architecturally and otherwise. You certainly have heard Sullivan's comment that the modern or contemporary world of architecture was delayed by about fifty years by the decisions of Mr. Burnham and the other architects, to linger with the classical tradition.

I have been trying to imagine what precisely would have happened if they had agreed with Louis Sullivan and decided on something original. Who would have been able to execute it?—except, of course, yourself. Would it really have changed things? Would the American people have caught on?

The ease with which you express yourself prompts me to hope that you recall something of interest to all of us. In any case, it would be nice to hear from you—and Rue and I are still looking forward to that long delayed visit to Taliesin.

Sincerely yours,
Al Shaw

July 11, 1953
Alfred Shaw
Chicago, Illinois

Dear Al,

Sullivan might still be alive.

I would have done several world fairs, government projects, and characterized the United States instead of the international style, etc., etc. The Chicago School would be in Europe instead of the Bauhaus in America, etc., etc.

Anyhow, come on—see us—anytime now.

October 3, 1956
Mr. Frank Lloyd Wright
Taliesin, Spring Green, Wisconsin

Re: Dinner and Exhibit in Honor of Louis Sullivan

Dear Mr. Wright:

As a memorial to "The Master," Louis Sullivan, the Art Institute and the Chicago Chapter of the A.I.A. are looking forward to your presence and a few remarks about him at the dinner to his honor at the Mayfair Room of the Sheraton-Blackstone Hotel in Chicago at 6:30 P.M. on October 24th. After the dinner, we will all review the exhibits of his work at the Art Institute. Our anticipated program will include:

Frank Lloyd Wright, Gold Medalist of the A.I.A. and recipient of many world honors.

Mies van der Rohe, F.A.I.A., whom Mr. Wright "gave to us" at a welcome meeting by the I.I.T. some years ago.

Daniel Catton Rich, Director of the Art Institute.

Dr. John Burchard, Dean of Humanities, Massachusetts Institute of Technology.

Mrs. Loucheim (Wife of Eero Saarinen) Art Critic, New York Times.

We are looking forward to the great pleasure of your being with us to do honor to Louis Sullivan.

Yours most sincerely,
William Jones Smith
For the Program Committee of the
Chicago Chapter, A.I.A.

October 4, 1956
Mr. William Jones Smith
Chicago, Illinois

Mr. dear William Smith:

The "Jones" in your name would bring me to the dinner with tears in my eyes. I am very largely Jones [his grandfather's name] and since I am a living tribute to my loving master I could not fail to bring my bouquet to lay on his bier while he is now being passed around.

October 26, 1956
Aline Loucheim Saarinen
Bloomfield Hills, Michigan

Dear Aline:

Here is apology for breaking down when I could rightfully be expected to contribute a telling note to the occasion as you did.

But it was either that or sobbing and I chose to swear—the male substitute for tears. I saw him die deserted and in awful misery—alone except for little but myself. I'll tell you about it sometime.

So please understand what you probably know already—and give my best hope to your Eero.

Affection,
Frank Lloyd Wright

II

IN THE CAUSE OF ARCHITECTURE

Upon leaving the office of Adler and Sullivan in 1893, Frank Lloyd Wright and his long-time friend Cecil Corwin set up a private practice in the Adler and Sullivan-designed Schiller Building in Chicago. Mr. Wright told us long afterward that when he was moving into his new office, the gilder came to put his name on the plate glass door. When the work was finished, the newly installed architect looked at the sign on the door which read: FRANK LLOYD WRIGHT: ARCHITECT, and immediately thought to himself: "My God, what nerve!"

That incident, and how he felt about it, was indicative of how highly he held the practice of architecture, not just as a mere profession, but as a great art, as a sacred obligation to design beautiful structures in which others would live and work.

His first commission was a house and stables for William H. Winslow of River Forest, a suburb of Chicago near Oak Park, where Mr. Wright had his own home and studio. He had known Mr. Winslow from the days of his work with Adler and Sullivan. Winslow, as head of Winslow Ornamental Iron Works, had come frequently to consult with Mr. Wright about iron work being done for the firm. Now he came as Mr. Wright's first client.

What Frank Lloyd Wright designed and built for William Winslow clearly took the form of a presentiment, a prophecy, of the work that was to follow. Certain elements in the house show influences of his time with Louis Sullivan, but these are confined to the terracotta frieze of the second story, its ornamental motif, and the use of arches on the porte-cochere. The overall design, however, possesses a grace and proportion that is decidedly Mr. Wright's own work. Decoration and ornament can be taught and learned, passed on and acquired. But an innate sense of proportion is a gift that accompanies genius. In the Winslow house and stables there is an unerring rightness that reveals the work not of a novice fulfilling his first commission but of a master in full possession of his capabilities.

Since his practice began with residential work, his earliest striking insights on the nature of his profession dealt with the homes that America was currently building.

"What was the matter with the kind of house I found on the prairie? Well, let me tell you in more detail. Just for a beginning, let's say that house lied about everything. It had no sense of Unity at all nor any such sense of space as should belong to a free man among a free people in a free country. It was stuck up and stuck on, however it might be done. Wherever it happened to be. To take any one of those so-called 'homes' away would have improved the landscape and cleared the atmosphere. It was a box, too, cut full of holes to let in light and air, an especially ugly one to get in and out of....My first feeling therefore had been a yearning for simplicity. A new sense of simplicity as 'organic.' This had barely begun to take shape in my mind when the Winslow house was planned. But now it began in practice."

It was clear that by the year 1900 his work was fully developed, having matured in the houses that sprang up across the Midwest prairie in and around Chicago, beginning with the Winslow residence in 1893.

From where we now stand in the twentieth century, it is difficult to gain a clear perspective of what Frank Lloyd Wright faced in the way of struggle in order to do work in the years 1900-1910. Everything in architecture was relegated to a category of "styles," and the more money and power the client had, the more "stylish" and "grand" his house must be. The conventional architects of the day simply read through the vast pages of past-built buildings. There was little or no creativity involved. As Louis Sullivan liked to say, satirizing how those style-book architects worked: "Boy, take down number 87 and put a bay window on it for the lady." Ever since the Renaissance, when architecture was dominated by the painter and the sculptor, architecture as the principal art had died. Buildings were conceived in elevation, as though they were pictures erected for human habitation.

*from Frank Lloyd Wright, *An Autobiography*, Horizon Press, 1977, New York.

In the early years of the twentieth century, a handful of architects working in Europe were trying to break away from the bondage of decoration and ornament, styles and fashions that had held sway for five centuries. These men included Karl Moser in Switzerland; Otto Wagner, Adolf Loos and Joseph Olbricht in Vienna; the deStyl group in Holland: J.J.P. Oud, H. Th. Widjeveld and H. P. Berlage; Henry Van der Velde in Belgium; Charles René MacIntosh in the British Isles; Erich Mendelsohn and Peter Behrens in Germany, to cite the principal ones. Their breakthrough concepts, however, and their implementation, came from Frank Lloyd Wright. As he was building across the Midwest prairie in those first years, he referred to his work as the "new" architecture. In it the concept of the structure came first from the plan, the arrangement of interior space. From the plan grew the elevation, as the result of that plan, and from a combination of the two evolved the third dimension. This third dimension, for Mr. Wright, meant "depth" both in a physical and philosophical meaning.

The most important single event in the history and growth of modern architecture in Europe was unquestionably the publication of the work *Ausgeführte Bauten und Entwürfe von Frank Lloyd Wright (The Completed Buildings and Projects of Frank Lloyd Wright)* by the noted publishing house of Ernst Wasmuth, in Berlin, 1910. Mr. Wright left his family, his studio, his practice behind him and traveled to Florence to prepare the drawings for the plates of this lavish and elegant two-folio monograph.

In the year 1911 the same publisher issued a photographic record of the constructed work of Frank Lloyd Wright, and these two publications, first the beautiful folio of plans and perspectives, and then an extensive collection of built buildings, became an elixir for the young architects of Europe. Their enthusiasm often found its way into print:

If it had not already been an established fact that Wright holds a place among the greatest architects of these times, then it could certainly be concluded from the influence he exercises. The two things that impressed me most during my visit to America were Wright's Larkin Building at Buffalo and the Niagara Falls."
                                        Dr. E. P. Berlage
                                        State Architect of Holland, 1917

"In my opinion the figure of Frank Lloyd Wright towers so assuredly above the surrounding world that I make bold to call him one of the very

greatest of our time without fearing that a later generation will have to reject the verdict."

J.J.P. Oud
City Architect, Rotterdam, 1919

"Who supports is fortunate; who leads is the chosen one. Such a chosen one is Frank Lloyd Wright. All his work is directed to that on which his mind so fondly dwells—the realization of a new civilization with an architecture of its own—which makes the machine its slave—and creates nobler longing for mankind and brings repose from prairie borders to the heart of the desert or from the mountains down to the boundless plain."

H. Th. Widjeveld
Architect, Editor of Wendingen, 1925

"Without doubt the strongest human document to prove and establish such faith as our present age possesses is the work of Frank Lloyd Wright. Mr. Wright's achievements are, in no respect, nationally bound. His work is a creative emancipation of humanity."

Professor H. DeFries
Dusseldorf, Germany, 1926

"Inexhaustible the richness of his form. The form-father of our modern life—his creation stands at the center of our time. Where yet is his equal to be found?"

Erich Mendelsohn
Architect, Berlin, 1929

The Wasmuth portfolio represented only some of his work from 1893 to 1909, beginning with the Winslow house and concluding with Como Orchards Summer Colony for Montana. But it did include two works that exerted the most influence: the Larkin Building (1903) and Unity Temple (1904). The Larkin Building was called by Mr. Wright "The Grammar of the Protestant," and sometimes "The Affirmative Negation," meaning that the building protested against the cliche of styles and forms that did not belong to the twentieth century, protested against the misuse of materials, protested against the application of inappropriate decoration that had no place in a modern building for the man of the new century.

He stripped the building of unnecessary ornament and replaced it with strong and simple forms: the sculptural massing of the very structure itself became its own "ornament." But for him the key element in conceiving a building was to create a third-dimensional structure, from within outward, the exterior form taking shape because of the space within. "Form Follows Function," Louis Sullivan used to say, but Mr. Wright believed that "Form and Function are One," the way the flower, the leaf, the stem, the root, are all together one.

This concern with what he came more and more to call "the destruction of the box in architecture" became a subject of many of his talks to the Taliesin Fellowship. On the evening of August 13, 1952, he spoke to us as follows:

"When the Larkin Building model was first brought into the studio, that stair tower at the corner was part of the mass, part of the building. And I didn't know what was the matter. I was trying for something with some freedom that I hadn't got. Suddenly, the model was standing on the studio table in the center, I came in and I saw what was the matter. I took those four corners and I pulled them out away from the building, made them individual features, planted them. And there began the thing that I was trying to do. You see, I got features instead of walls. I followed that up with Unity Temple where there were no walls of any kind, only features; and the features were screens grouped about interior space. The thing that came to me by instinct in the Larkin Building began to come consciously in Unity Temple.

"When I finished Unity Temple, I had it. I was conscious of the idea. I knew I had the beginning of a great thing, a great truth in architecture. And now architecture could be free."

The "great truth in architecture" he chose to call Organic Architecture." Organic architecture meant, for him, that all the parts are related to each other, and in turn all related to the whole—no more cut-up spaces with unrelated ornamentation. He also believed in the integrity of materials and used each material according to its inherent nature: wood he treated as wood, brick as brick, stone as stone, likewise steel, glass, concrete. And he believed profoundly in the individual, in the human being, and thus in the use of what he called "human scale" in whatever building he created. A building, then, must be of its own time and place, a twentieth century work constructed and made possible by twentieth century materials and methods, for twentieth century man.

To his dismay, however, he saw his work coming back to him distorted in the buildings being done by the new Bauhaus architects and others in Europe. He realized that the most important message of his work had been "lost in translation." Where the space within had become the great reality for him, forever evident in any building he would ever design, the new architecture of Europe was form-oriented at the expense of integrity. To make a clear differentiation between his work and theirs, he used the phrase "Organic Architecture." He would spend a lifetime building, defining, and defending Organic Architecture.

The letters in this second section trace the constant and continuing struggle on his part to make his work understood, to communicate his vision on its own terms to a world, particularly his own corner of it, that preferred to accept a fragment of that vision instead of the whole. For him, the International Style lacked the third dimension, depth. It had reverted, despite its use of twentieth century terms, to the old emphasis on facaded architecture that Europe had been steeped in since the Renaissance.

Many of the architects to whom he wrote these letters were also his personal friends: Raymond Hood, Mies van der Rohe, Eliel Saarinen, J.J.P. Oud, Mendelsohn, Philip Johnson—there are many others. His sense of friendship colors his correspondence with them, even in the midst of bitter quarrels. But his first loyalty, early and late, was to the Organic Architecture he loved with all his heart and which he protected, at times ferociously. Just as his buildings were true to the sites on which they arose, so he remained true to his architectural ideal. Always, throughout his long and brilliantly productive career he continued his crusade for Organic Architecture. It was the underlining constant, the guiding principle of his genius. In one of his many talks to us at Taliesin he reiterated his deep belief in the concept of Principle—especially as it related to the cause of architecture for future generations:

"As beautiful building after beautiful building gets itself constructed and built, they [the future generations] will begin to look into it and try to find out what the secret was that kept it perennially young, always working, and never let die, because it couldn't die. You see, a Principle never dies."

February 24, 1915
Wilhelm Miller
Los Angeles, California

This letter, despite its convoluted sequence, is an important one, because it introduces most of the key concepts that Mr. Wright will defend and amplify throughout the rest of his life, namely:
1. the creative individual as opposed to the group

2. *the "organic nature" of architecture*
3. *the nature of Midwestern (prairie) America*
4. *the integrity of Principle*
5. *the ideal of a truly American culture.*

My dear Mr. Wilhelm Miller:

In answer to your question No. 1:
I am unwilling to wear any tag which will identify me with any sect or system.

The fact that "a university could not lay itself open to the charge of accepting the work of a single man" is one of the things that makes a university either a "dead letter" or a "useless striving to deliver man from system by means of systems," as Blake puts it; a drag upon the vitality of the country instead of truly conservative of progressive force.

Question No. 2:
Of the fundamental idea or motive impulse behind the work of the group you mention as the "school" you would name, I confess myself perplexed. So far I have seen little to convince me that that work is in itself in that connection a product peculiar to a group. I believe that it will become such a product in time because some of the men at least who are now using forms not their own would not concern themselves with them unless the true sentiment for what is behind those forms had been awakened in them.

Louis Sullivan, so far as any knowledge I have of him goes, never thought or cared about the prairie as an influence in his art and I cannot see how he could figure in any form other than grotesque as the founder of a "Prairie School of Architecture." Mr. Sullivan preached in words and as well as he could in his work that "form should follow function" in architecture as in life, which is precisely what form has always done wherever it arose as an expression with the dignity of great art. But it is language merely, at best knowledge only, until it is realized in works, and that realization seems to be the difficulty just now.

Mr. Sullivan gave to us out of his experience a great achievement as his distinct contribution to the architecture of our time, and that gift was the "skyscraper" as a unified thing—as *one* beautiful building instead of several ugly ones piled one on top of another. He *realized* the *nature* of the thing and gave to it the expression which he conceived as belonging to it, and so a new thing took its place in the sun. I do not know what that has to do with the prairie or a "Prairie School of Architecture," unless inspired by his example, or by the organic nature of his effort, other men gathered into themselves the nature of the prairie, the life lived upon it and the tools at hand with which to work: then with individual feeling for a unity that they perceived might be, proceeded to realize it in works, the forms of which expressed in character and spirit that nature, forms that were *invented by these men.*

I have early recorded the confession that I tried to do this. What I have accomplished will speak for itself eventually. No university, especially no American university, will speak for it until the work is strong enough to require nothing of the university. German universities and the Imperial University of Japan have already given it recognition.

Question No. 3:

As to a specific "School of Architecture," Marcus Aurelius may answer: "Judge every word and deed which are according to nature to be fit for thee, and be not diverted by the blame which follows from any people nor by their words, but if a thing is good to be done or said, do not consider it unworthy of thee, for those who would blame or praise thee have their own peculiar leading principle and follow that peculiar leading principle and follow their peculiar movement, which things do not thou regard but go straight on following thy own nature and the way of both is one."

Question No. 4:

The first important work which recognized artistically the influence of the prairie was, so far as I know, the Winslow House, designed in 1893, and the dedication to the prairie of the types that followed was published first, I believe, in a number of the Architectural Record of New York especially devoted to my work. I think it was the March number of 1908; I wrote the text myself. An earlier publication of the Architectural Review of Boston (I think it was in 1898) had an earlier phase of the work, for which Robert Spencer, who had become my friend, wrote the text. I have no copy of the Record myself and none is to be obtained except from some subscriber who is willing to loan or part with a copy. The University Library probably has one on file.

Question No. 5:

This article in the Record is the one to which I refer in the first sentence of "Studies and Executed Buildings." I have acknowledged the influence of the prairie in developing the forms I have used and dedicated the types to the prairie, but I have never used the phrase, "Prairie Style of Architecture."

I hope, my dear Mr. Miller, that these brief answers will give you what you want. You are doing good work, I think, in running these things down or setting them up in scholarly fashion.

To go back again to your remark in question No. 1—I am sorry that an *American* university should feel that the work of a man is only worthy of university recognition and support when it has got far enough along to be recognized as the work of many, loses its individual distinction and becomes a matter of "the group." I believe it is the same old so-called "conservatism" that leaves the crux of progress to take care of itself and instead of walking hopefully abreast of the times is content to walk behind. When this following behind is a rear guard action in the case of a retreating civilization, it may be truly conservative, but when it is only reticence or a fear to prejudice the mediocre-many or is a distrust of the soundness of its own judgment and this when the movement of the times is forward-double-quick, it seems to me not conservative in any true sense. Certainly it has not been and so perhaps we need another type of educational institution in this country at this stage of development, one in front as well as one behind.

Sincerely your Friend,
Frank Lloyd Wright

November 30, 1922
Jacobus Johann Pieter Oud
Rotterdam, Holland

My dear Architect Oud,

A postal card reached me in Japan with a warm expression of appreciation of your visit to my mother in Oak Park.

Upon my arrival home from the Orient I find your kind letter. I take the liberty of enclosing a likeness of myself made five years ago as a token of appreciation of your personal worth and would appreciate one of yourself—if you care to send it to me. This is a *Japanese* rather than an *American* custom and not at all European—nevertheless your interest and kindness moves me to send it and ask for yours. I hope someday to see you.

I am sending to you a small collection of views of some later work which I ask you to study and pass on to Dr. Berlage whose criticism in Wendingen has just been read to me by one of your countrymen, Bosch-Reitz of the Metropolitan Museum in New York.

The publication reached me just by accident—no one in Holland sending one to me. It is the most interesting presentation of half-tones I have ever seen, the grey running patterns of each page holding the illustrations well into the whole scheme.

If you will forward also to Dr. Berlage the enclosed note and the pamphlet (which I beg you to read) together with the photographs so soon as you would have done with them, I will be much obliged to you. I do not have nor can I find his address. And also another favor—I have no copies of these photographs at hand. And I have several earnest requests from the Tchecoslowaquie for photographs and essays coming via Bedrich Feuerstein, Umlecka Beseda, Prague II, Jungmanova 36. If you will request Dr. Berlage—which I have neglected to do in the letter just written—to send on the photographs and the pamphlet too (which is my only spare copy) for them to read and return to him—I shall be infinitely obliged to both of you.

You may say to him that any use he cares to make of the photographs or text he is welcome to make, and the same applies to yourself. I will write to Mr. Feuerstein that all the available material I have at present is in your hands and will be in a short time forwarded to him.

This rather awkward way of imposing myself upon you and upon Dr. Berlage, I hope you will overlook—as it is the first time in my life I have sent a photograph of myself to anyone or myself sent any photographs of my work to anyone—except the Schweizerich-Beurzeitung on the occasion of Dr. Berlage's recital of his experiences in America. I also failed to meet him as I was then in Japan at work, as I was when you came to America.

Since I hope to come to Europe and shall avail myself of your kind invitation, I shall look you up and ask you to introduce me to the young men in Architecture in Holland.

I should be grateful for Dr. Berlage's address. I take it that yours is Schiedamke Weg but am not sure.

I will again write the Prague address:

Bedrich Feuerstein
Umlecka Beseda
Prague II Jungmanova 36
Tchecoslowaquie Europa

I do not myself keep much in touch with current work or architects here and subscribe to no Architectural Magazines whatever, unless I do now subscribe to Wendingen which I intend to do. So you see I can't much help you in your quest. I am sorry not to be able to do so. I may be able to give you some information when I come to Europe as I hope to do this winter.

Meantime, believe me, gratefully yours,

November 30, 1922
Dr. Hendrick Petrus Berlage
Amsterdam, Holland

Mr dear Dr. Berlage,

A copy of "Wendingen" with an article by yourself appreciative of my work has reached me, quite by chance.

During the past five years I have been much in Japan—in fact, most of the time. I missed you when you visited America. I have been unable to respond to a number of appeals from the young men of Holland—doubtless regarding this issue of Wendingen. Had I been aware of the seriousness of their purpose, however, I might have responded with more characteristic views of my later work to be included in their publication. I hope to come to Europe soon and will give myself the pleasure of seeking you in Amsterdam, or wherever you may be at that time. I would like to reply to some of your friendly queries expressed in Wendingen as read to me by a countryman of yours, Bosch-Reitz of the Metropolitan Museum of New York City.

Yes, you are right. I have been romancing—engaged upon a great Oriental Symphony—when my own people should have kept me at home busy with their own characteristic industrial problems—work which I would really prefer to do and I have done.

But, dear Dr. Berlage, I am branded as an "Artist" architect, and so under suspicion by my countrymen—and especially as I have been an "insurgent" in private life as well as in my work; and my hair is not short nor my clothes so utterly conventional as to inspire confidence in the breast of the good American Business Man that I am a good "business proposition." It costs more to employ me—it's a matter [of] imposing independent thought and action and some pains upon the man who employs me. It is difficult to achieve "the greater end," and part of that difficulty is the client's. So I have had to go where opportunity led me, and I have had very little choice. However I assure you my heart is still where it was in 1908 in the article I then wrote—the only remaining copy of which I send you—it is a reprint. The originals are no longer to be had and my own is all marked up by notations and corrections made by myself. I do not know if you have read it over. It says pretty much what I would say today.

I am not discouraged—but what encouragement I receive comes chiefly from Europe from men like yourself who have the benefit of a more cultured background, and from the younger men of my own country who begin restlessly to realize the emptiness of imitation—but who unfortunately turn too easily to a fresh model for imitation rather than to the *principles* that are eternal and forever fruitful.

For this reason there is much talk now of a "School"—the "New School of the Middle West"—and if the work of a master—Louis H. Sullivan—that stands by itself and the work of a pupil (myself) that stands now by itself can be stretched to cover the group of imitators and pupils who take refuge in this allegation of a "School" then perhaps we, too, may speak of a new School in Architecture in America. I am slow to do so because only evidence that the *principles* I advocate are being realized would convince me—and this, frankly, I do not see. But this may be only the preliminary stage of the real thing to come. I hope so. It is difficult to see in our own day the values of current events—we lack perspective. I am looking forward to meeting you and talking over these and other matters so intimate and dear to us all as serious minded architects and toward meeting the young men of Holland whose vitality and purpose is evident as I look over the numbers of Wendingen loaned me by a friend and I remember a young man, Van T. Hoff, who was filled with high purpose when I met him here seven or eight years ago, whom I expect to find has done some good things. Your own work I am anxious to see. I wish to thank you simply and sincerely for your able minded and generous criticism of my work. Good criticism is itself creative and needed by my country more than anything else. We have not enough of the critical spirit.

A separate packet will bring you a few photographs of the Barnsdall House and a few views of the then finished portion of the "Oriental Symphony" in Tokyo. I would like to go through that vast building with you some time—and I enclose a description and an editorial written there at the time which will explain in a measure the nature of the building and the undertaking. The Japanese seemed enthusiastic and grateful but were being subjected to criticisms of every kind and nationality—the British being the only ones adverse except countrymen of my own.

I send these things not as having any critical value but merely as all I have just now to indicate something of the nature of the thing done as the layman there sees it. Any photographs you may care to send me regarding your own work, I should most pleased to receive. Please accept this letter as a token of my esteem and appreciation and interest in you good self—we have a common cause—and a common interest.

Sincerely yours,

January 7, 1925
H. Th. Widjeveld
Oosterbeek, Holland

My dear Herr Widjeveld,

I am at last sending the long promised material. I started to make suggestions in the "dummy" Wendingen but soon gave it up, leaving it all to you. I should like a very dignified cover—featuring the red square perhaps. (Since writing this we have worked out a scheme here, which we submit for your approval.)

I think you will find some material you will prefer to use instead of some of the Chicago houses like the Baldwin and Bach, etc.

I suggest you use a double-page plan of Taliesin in place of the two details of same already published.

It would be nice to have a touch of color in the volume to give the color sense of the Midway Gardens and the Imperial, and I have sent the color drawings for that purpose. But it is up to you.

I have sent the actual working plans, thinking you could photograph them directly and half-tone them to good advantage. They are thus authentic.

I have included some of the personal sketches for details of the Imperial and a few other things. I enclose some photos of the architect himself for you to choose from.

I have written an article for you,
      "In the Cause of Architecture"
      "For Wendingen with an Appendix addressed 'To my European Colleagues'"
Mr. Sullivan's articles on the Imperial are the best to introduce in that connection and I enclose them.
I have also sent descriptions of the Larkin Building, Unity Temple, the Coonley House, the California work—which may go in separately where appropriate. It is not necessary to use these at all—unless you wish.

I think Berlage's article as translated needs a little editing. I have made so bold, as I think the word "knack" is not what he meant if he understood English precisely. It is rather a low word. I've lost the last page—but you have one no doubt.

I hope the work may be expedited and the drawings promptly returned. I can't tell you how much I dislike to let them go out of the country. They will be needed here early in February for an exhibition at the Chicago Art Institute which may continue among European countries.

I feel that this Wendingen publication can not fail to be valuable as the first authentic publication of work done since 1909 and the only one on an artistic scale of any importance. So here's hoping for your success at an early date. I am sorry to be so late but important work has kept me very busy and it is got óff to you with difficulty and in haste even now.

My sincerest regards to you. I enjoyed Erich Mendelsohn's visit very much. Thank you for sending him.

Sincerely yours,

I am sending a series of line drawings of the Midway Gardens which I would like to see reproduced across double pages—as the Gardens are to be destroyed before long. And this will be a record of what they once were. The drawings are accurate and excellent.

You will have a wealth of material to choose from to make this one of the most interesting of architectural publications. A sort of exhibit in itself.

I have sent to DeFries in Berlin for reproductions in color, in two portfolio monographs, two recent projects, one at Los Angeles and one at Lake Tahoe, which could not possibly be got into Wendingen and are not executed, as I have promised him material he has anxiously awaited long since.

I think, the Wendingen should be pushed so as not to be behind these things of DeFries if possible.

October 30, 1925
H. Th. Widjeveld
Oosterbeek, Holland

My dear Herr Widjeveld,

The first *Heft* of Wendingen came at last and was a pleasant thing to see. "Some Flowers for Architect FLlW" was a charming and graceful compliment of highest value and I hope some day to be able to return it in some fashion.

This first volume has of course only material well-known already—but it shows the scale and character of the completed whole in a way convincing to those who know what material is available—but only to those.

Kroch of Chicago has undertaken 500 copies so soon as I showed him the sample copy, but expressed the opinion (which I share) that if the work would be shown in its entirety some 2,000 copies might easily be sold in America. As additional numbers come out the interest will increase.

Kroch has written to Mees—and I have ordered 100 copies to put away against some future time.

I hope there will be some plates to indicate the color of the work—in subsequent numbers.

I am in need of the material as soon as possible—the original matter, I mean—and hope you will send it as soon as possible. Herman Sorgel from Munich has just been here (in Chicago) but I was not at home and so missed him. He said, in a note, he had seen the copy of Wendingen and was anxious to get out a number which he thought would surpass it in quality of workmanship! I must say the Wendingen however seems pretty good to me.

I have had your request for "To My European Colleagues" in mind but could find no record of that article. Am enclosing herewith another if you care to use it. It is of a more philosophical sort, and it may have been better to talk of walls and beams and schemes of construction and methods of design. However it may be interesting as showing the simple faith that encourages the work to go on in spite of discouragement.

I hope all is well with you and you may be coming here yourself before long and we shall have you as guest at Taliesin for some time. And if there is a Mrs. Widjeveld we should want her also.

Kindly advise me as to the progress of the work and as to anything I can do to help forward [it].

I am working on a great commercial building, a copy of a photograph of the perspective drawing enclosed—but not for publication yet. A new system of cantilevered floor construction—resting on *interior* pylons extending from 60 feet below ground to above the building as you see, where the set-back occurs. The exterior is a screen all of copper and glass carried from floor to floor on the cantilever projections of the floors—a projection from the pylons of twelve feet all around. This shell or screen is a mechanized fabric some four or five inches thick and deducts nothing from rentable ground area as the glass is on the lot-line, and continuous. The fire escapes are integral stairways between floors (see center of each unit). There is nothing in the way of the commercial uses of the various floors—and nothing manufactured as features for effect. All is enclosed commercial space with clear outside glass.

My best to you with a hope to meet and talk with you—soon.

Willitts House

Larkin Building

Larkin Building, interior

Unity Temple

Unity Temple, interior

Frank Lloyd Wright, 1908

Coonley House

Coonley House, interior

Robie House

Taliesin, overview

Taliesin

Concert in the Taliesin Living Room, Christmas, 1924

Left to right: Frank Lloyd Wright, Richard Neutra, Sylva Moser, Kameki and Nobu Tsuchiura, Werner Moser, Dione Neutra

December 8, 1928
Mr. Jens Jensen
Ravinia, Illinois

My dear Jens:

How nasty mean you are! You've written me three letters now all about Jews, snakes, and dried herring hanging beneath your eaves, of which I am supposed, I suppose, to be one. I thought you and Mrs. Jensen said goodbye to me very nicely.

One bright spot in your letter was the Jensen admiration of Mrs. Wright. With all that you say of her, I agree. As for myself, don't grieve too soon Jens, and don't worry at all.

Like in all arguments we all meant practically the same thing. It is never possible to bring out the meaning of any subjective matter without being rehearsed in the language—in being sure that all are speaking the same language. The only difference between Olgivanna and myself is that she believes that the creative instinct is the original birthright of mankind and in most of them it lies dead—in any case paralysed and that by proper treatment it may be revived. I too believe that creative-faculty is the birthright of Man—the quality which enabled him to distinguish himself from the brute, but that owing to his betrayal of himself, the tricks which he has played upon himself with his brain, what he calls his intellect—and by means of his arrogant presumptions, abstractions, all turned into a system of so called education, he has sterilized himself. And I believe that now not only is this creative-instinct dead in most, but it has ceased to exist at all, to such an extent that perhaps three fifths of humanity lacks any power of that kind. Now I believe the creative instinct in Man is that quality or faculty in him of getting himself reborn and born again—of getting himself born into everything that he does, everything that he really works with. By means of it he has got the gods if not God. It is his imagination that is chiefly the tool with which this force or faculty in him works. By putting a false premium upon will and intellect he has done this injury upon himself—he has worked this injury upon himself.

Now how to get it back—this quality of Man—back again to men. How to preserve what little there is glimmering of it in whatever human being it may be glimmering in. Our first concern about that should be the first thought of every thinking man in our country today.

And that Jens, is why I am interested in this proposed school. I should like to be one to initiate steps that would put a little experimental station at work where this thing might be wooed and won, if only to a small extent. I know it cannot be taught.

No doubt what you mean by "dried-up" and being "hooked" is what you imagine to be the exorbitant egotism of the man who arrogates to himself creative power and denies it to most. Very well. Hypocrisy has many good and desirable features—modesty is among them, chivalry too. Where people live much together, these things are essential. But men "dry up" from the inhibition which imposes these things upon the ego. Those who allow the ego a natural scope and insist on the privileges and rights due to the equality of man he may feel working in him are wiser—Walt Whitman foremost among these. Of course Jens, that man will be most beloved who concedes most to his fellow man, who will make the grandest gestures and say the things he knows his fellow man likes to see and hear about himself. But there is a wholesome candor more valuable in any final analysis, conspicuously lacking in any such democracy as ours and while I have no less faith in man than any or all of my opponents in this long-lasting argument of ours, I have less faith in men. And I am for taking steps—constructive steps—*now*, not sometimes, to save the precious quality which is the soul of man himself, from further atrophy, from greater degradation at his own hands. So I am no singer for this false sentimentalized American democracy. I see the evil consequence all too plainly of this making a god of Demos—of this patting of the common-denominator on the back and ascribing to it the virtues of deity.

It is so common now, for political reasons, as to be nauseating and the hypocrisy necessary to it as a view of life and for conduct so imbued in the man as to be like the color of his hair, the shape of his nose, or the timbre of his voice.

So, anomaly though it may seem to you Jens, as I love Man more, I grow to love men less. Now this may be the result—the reaction—of a too violent contact with the pretenses and the hypocrisy of a half-based opportunist democracy, busy feathering its own nest at the expense of all the nobler virtues. I may swing back, in time, into the marching column, but when I do, the column will be marching in the right direction, and to the proper tune. That tune is the over-word and they will be willing to take it as their watchword.

Hope to see you soon again. Meantime

Faithfully yours,

December 13, 1928
Mr. Albert W. Kelsey
Philadelphia, Pa.

My dear Albert Kelsey:

Your recent letters have taken me back to the time when the Architectural League of America had its meetings in Chicago when I first made your acquaintance.

I have always had you in mind as a most agreeable, potent and valuable person. We had both lived to see great changes take place in architecture, and your enthusiasm for my old Meister Louis Sullivan is amply justified at this moment when the ideals that he and I stood for almost alone at that time are now sweeping the country and in danger of becoming a French fashion.

But, dear man, I have never entered a competition. I disbelieve in them so strongly. I have never known anything to come out of competition in a way of a building or any other work of art that was not mediocre. A competition is an average of averages, upon averages, for averages. How could anything distinguished survive that? While you assure me that inasmuch as thirty or forty designs are to be published mine are almost sure to be included, even that, dear Kelsey, is not good enough. I suppose I might do something highly imaginative as you say, and it might entertain your committee and concerning which you personally might be enthusiastic, but I should have to lay aside actual work to do it and frankly, I don't feel that I would be justified. Were I sufficiently distinguished, and the members of your committee sufficiently interested in what I might do, in the light of what I have done in the past, to say to me and several others concerning whom they might have a similar feeling, "Come now, we are interested in your work. We believe you could do something for us worth while. Lay aside your projects long enough to show us what you can do for us. We will pay you for your trouble whether we use your design or whether we do not." Then I should feel respected, justly compensated, and interested. Something might come of that. But I suspect that no one will ever see my name attached to any work submitted in a public competition no matter how interesting or how great the price.

The only thing that makes this competition work different from all other competitions is the fact of your presence in it or rather your connection with it. If anything could induce me break with principle, it would be that fact. But even that is not enough. If you come this way to Chicago, let me know. I should like a visit with you at Taliesin—my workshop and home.

If the old fund of enthusiasm for the beautiful and your abundant faith in high ideals is still untarnished, we could have a happy time. Reading your Pan American program, I should judge that this was true.

July 24, 1929
Mr. R. M. Schindler
Los Angeles, California

My dear Rudolph Schindler:

Concerning your application for a license to the Board of Architects in California, I wrote a letter to the Board (some years ago, now, I believe), recommending you as a competent architect from my standpoint, entirely entitled to a license to build anything anywhere in this country. But since that was insufficient and more is required, let me be specific.

I am in receipt of a letter from the Board asking if you had made designs for me. The answer to that is—No you didn't. Nobody makes designs for me. Sometimes if they are in luck, or rather if I am in luck, they make them with me.

Nevertheless, I believe that you now are competent to design exceedingly good buildings. I believe that anything you would design would take rank in the new work being done in the country as worthy of respect.

They mentioned that they wanted to know also what you did with me in connection with the Imperial Hotel in Tokyo. You worked on the structure and on the architectural plans for the Imperial Hotel. The fact that these plans were all thrown away when I got to Japan and I built the building myself out of the office there is no reflection upon the work that you and the other men concerned did in that connection.

I am willing to make affidavit that I consider you competent to calculate structures and make good plans either on your own, or for anyone else.

As for class A construction, it is poor enough. If, after your experience with me and the unusual intelligence which I believe you to possess, you could not improve upon the problems arising in class A construction current in Los Angeles, I should say something had happened to you to make you unworthy of your association with myself.

Now it may be that your architectural relation with me is against you. I doubt this. I do not know of anything I have done to lower the level of the architectural standards of Los Angeles. I do not know of anything I have done or would do to insult my brother architects there. But I do not see why it is necessary for me to subscribe to their view in the practice of architecture in order to have their respect. Nor for you to do so either.

It is hard for me to believe them so illiberal or so prejudiced that they would not allow any man so competent as yourself to stand shoulder to shoulder with them in putting Los Angeles on the architectural map of these United States.

July 25, 1929
Werner Moser
Zurich, Switzerland

Dear Werner:

A charmingly affectionate letter from Endo San from Tokyo has set me thinking about my boys in the various parts of this little world and naturally I thought about you and Sylva and the babies and the new one just arrived. And then I realized I owed you several letters. Olgivanna, I believe, has been giving you news meantime.

Taliesin is again going and younger and, I am glad to say, more beautifully kept than ever before.

There are six boys here with me now, and a Japanese boy is on the way. One from Cologne, one of Schneider's pupils from Hamburg, one piano-player from Prague, one who has been through the mill here in America for four or five years—a Bavarian—a young American Armour graduate, and a young American who has been the round of the plan factories.

We were all in Arizona last winter in camp there, a view or two of a corner or two of which is enclosed. There are fifteen buildings in all, another—temporary—Taliesin in the great Desert. We shall be working there several winters leaving here about November 1st, returning about May 1st each year.

I've heard of you indirectly as doing things but nothing definite. Tell me about your work in hand and prospective.

I've enclosed a photo of the "San Marcos-in-the-Desert" which will be executed in the block system, texture as shown in the photograph of model herewith.

The country over here seems to be waking up.

"Mama Switzerland sleeps? Psst! Do not waken her," Werner. You see she will come around in time as Usonia [Mr. Wright's name for America] is coming.

Look at the Architectural Record for July. The Arizona Biltmore for one thing, and at the back, among Notes and Comments, my first comeback to all this "Surface and Mass" business of Corbusier et al. You ought to enjoy it. The war is on, I guess.

Somewhere I saw a church-tower I admired very much. Yes, at Basle, Professor K. Moser. Am I wrong in believing your father did it? The book in which I saw it is Onderdonk's "The Ferro Concrete Style." That tower and the church are fine pieces of work. Remember me to him with respect as nearly everything to date is in this book. You ought to have it.

We often speak of you and Sylva. Sylva always seemed a rare, fine spirit to us both and (as Endo said of a boy he is sending over) "good as much as she looked."

I suppose, the world being after all so very little, we'll all see each other again.

I'm getting whiter on top—I suppose I'm older than when we last met—but really, like the darky-girl who got married—her mistress soon afterward said to Lisa, "How do you like being married?" Said Lisa, "Oh mah goodness gracious, goodness, Ah don' see no diffunce." I don't see any difference yet, myself, but I was sixty the eighth of last June and am not going to allow birthdays anymore.

My three girls—Olgivanna, Svetlana, and Iovanna are with me everywhere. We have a beautiful new Packard sport-model open car and tour a great deal. Olgivanna and I drive 50 — 50. We drove in from Arizona, drove on to New York via Buffalo. Drove back via Baltimore and Springfield. We have two Dodge broughams for the boys.

I am trying to revive Hillside as an Art School with the help of the University.

There has been no *sensationalizing* for quite some time. Things are becoming peaceful and probably prosperous.

My love to you and yours. I am really very fond of you and Sylva. Taliesin has hardly been the same since the Moser's left, and the Tsuchiuras too.

Olgivanna joins me in best wishes, and congratulations on account of your growing "posterity."

August 7, 1929
Mr. Rudolph Schindler
Los Angeles, California

Dear Rudolph:

Here goes for a third try!
And I presume the letter would better be directed to the Board itself
as I had a letter here from them putting the question to me directly.
Samples enclosed to choose from.

Affectionately,

The Board of Architects of Southern California
Los Angeles, California

Gentlemen:

It's a damn'd shame that you fellows have refused Schindler a license
all these years.
He is worth any ten of you and he would be justified, were he sitting
where you sit, that is, sitting "blessed with a little brief authority," in refusing you a license to practice anything but draughting in some old-
fashioned architect's office.

Most respectfully yours,

The Board of Architects of Southern California
Los Angeles, California

Gentlemen:

Some time ago I received a letter from you inquiring about the
capacities of Mr. Rudolph Schindler of Kings Road, Los Angeles.
Some years ago, as you probably know, Mr. Schindler was one of the
men in my office. He had received good architectural training in Europe
and before coming to me had worked with an architect or two in our
own country. He seemed to have a good feeling for design and con-

siderable competence in making the calculations that go into the building of the modern structure.

When I left for Japan to build the Imperial Hotel, he remained in charge of the buildings there in Los Angeles which were going on at that time.

Since then he has built quite a number of buildings in and around Los Angeles that seem to me admirable from the standpoint of design, and I have not heard of any of them falling down.

I do not know that my opinion in this connection would be of any great value to the Board, but from my standpoint, he is entirely competent to design and build admirable buildings and I should unhesitatingly recommend him in that connection.

I am, gentlemen,

Sincerely yours,

The Board of Architects of Southern California
Los Angeles, California

Dear Sirs:

Mr. Rudolph Schindler, whom I have occasion to know well, desires to be legitimatized as a Los Angeles Architect. For some personal reasons I believe, for seven years the Board has refused his prayers in this connection.

During that time he has thrown no bombs, been guilty of neither licentious nor seditious conduct, except in refusing to have his hair cut or to dress well in conformity to the current fashion.

He has a good mind, is affectionate in disposition, and is fairly honorable I believe. Personally, though strongly individual, he is not unduly eccentric and I, in common with many others, like him very much.

Should you, however, be especially concerned with his qualifications as an architect, I know them to be many. He is a good draftsman, can calculate anything an architect should calculate. He is a competent designer. He has himself in the past seven years built many buildings that will take rank in respect to design, with any being built anywhere.

I can see no good reason whatever why he should not be legitimatized if he so desires it.

I am,

Respectfully yours,

December 12, 1929
Charles Morgan
Chicago, Illinois

Dear Charles:

Again I forgot to frame the letter which outlines the basis of our relations to each other on any work we may do together. I have never entered into any partnership agreement and probably never shall, being totally unfitted for that type of co-operation. I prefer "association," and am glad to have you as my Chicago-associate to help advance the work in that big city, and to share with me the responsibilities and rewards that come in the execution of whatever contracts we may have there.

This would leave specific arrangements as to the profits which may arise from Chicago work to be made, in each case, satisfactory to us. For instance, in the matter of the *Carl Schurz Memorial,* I had it in mind that I would make the preliminary sketch, and the preliminary fee for doing so would come to me in order that I might be then financed to proceed with the making of the plans, and also as an honorarium for the scheme and ideas involved. Then the plans should be made here in my workshop. After deducting the cost of engineers' services and the plan-making the balance of the fee which we would receive from our clients in this instance would be equally divided between us. In this particular case I should expect you to handle the superintendence and such business matters as you would be able to handle there in Chicago during the progress of the work. In this case it might be necessary to employ a building superintendent in addition to your own services. I am, of course, willing to give all the assistance I can give in the promotions you would undertake.

It would be part of our understanding that should any work come to me directly in Chicago we would make a similar arrangement modifying the terms somewhat, and should any work come directly to you, you would share it with me on a similar basis satisfactory to us both.

I suppose, after all, it is a partnership agreement, but a very free one, leaving us to tackle each problem and settle it between us as it arises, treating each on its merits as we proceed. In-as-much as I maintain the establishment here in the country for the making of plans, and travel to and fro to keep the work up in Chicago, it is not too much to expect that you maintain a modest establishment there in Chicago for interviewing and handling the business side of the execution of these projects.

In a general way, this seems to be the picture as I see it. Of course, many details will arise which I am sure can be worked out without any friction or serious disagreement between us. I have an associate in New York City, one in Phoenix, Arizona, one in Los Angeles, and may have others, but the field in Chicago seems gigantic enough to give you scope to all your energies; perhaps mine too, for that matter—eventually. You will be free to carry on your work of rendering for other architects so that the "pot" may be "kept boiling." Eventually however, as your interests with me naturally develop, I should think all your energies may be devoted to the duties and opportunities of Frank Lloyd Wright, Incorporated.

I should mention, I think, that our fees for such service as it would be necessary to render in condition with this work would be higher than customary—invariably 10 percent of the complete cost of the building—engineering included—2 1/2 percent in each case representing the so-called preliminary fee. All contracts should be made and plans too, in the name of Frank Lloyd Wright, Incorporated: Charles Morgan, Chicago Association.

It is now up to you to say what you think.

June 2, 1930
Raymond Hood
New York City, N.Y.

Dear Raymond,

I can't begin to express my admiration for your sportsmanship nor my liking for yourself. The visit to your home will be a pleasure to remember—always.

As for the dinner—well—there will not be many occasions like that one, we'll be talking about it once in a while all our lives, won't we?

I am back again "on the green" with my three girls—the birds singing—the gardens thriving—wondering if I am not something of a traitor to the great cause as I think of you fellows sweating away among the skyscrapers trying to do good things.

I might, by seniority, be helpful to all of you in some consultant or critical capacity, in connection with a "modern Architecture that would be genuine help in taking the lead that ought to be ours and is...I am thinking of the proposed fair." If it was in your cards to directly call on me in some such capacity before it is too late—more helpful probably than in building some particular building for you according to specification in some nook of the grounds as you suggested I would be called upon to do. But I suppose that matter is already foregone in the hands of Harvey Corbett "at the bat."

I might be a good umpire—if by any chance the realization that one was needed—should dawn. At any rate I hope we are not going to have another 30 years "set-back" by exaggerations of "ponderosity" for new patterns—for the foolish.

July 29, 1930
Arata Endo
Tokyo, Japan

My dear Endo,

It is a heroic performance and I can well imagine how much you put into it.

A Little-Imperial has been born in Japan...Hayashi San at last comes into his own. I am glad.

We must all admire his pluck and wish him financial and every other kind of success. You have courage and great promise, Endo San.

The amount of hard work you have put into the building no one can realize so well as I can...nor appreciate more, the charming ideas of which there are so many, nor realize so fully where your precedent led you astray.

Your building ends on the side of *exaggeration*. The Imperial was headed that way—in some respects. It is well never to make a feature of any kind for effects—independent of function?

The projecting slab as a motive in the Imperial was the floor—slab itself carried out for counter-balance and continuity. Then I got to playing with it a little for its own sake and that was where I "slopped over." That should stop right where I left it.

Nevertheless, my dear Endo, you've done your precedent proud in so many respects that you are sure to have great results from it in Japan...and how earnestly I hope you may.

Where in the world did Hayashi San get all the money? It must have cost a million yen at least?

For sumptuous effect I liked the rich cave-like interior at the ends of the Banquet Hall—a lovely idea.

I like your light towers too. The furniture (except the chairs in the bar, in which I seem to see Hayashi's hand?) is excellent—though the bedrooms seem a little over furnished—and the carpets "weak."

I could wish you had put the plans under your arm and come over for a conference. I think I could have saved you so much by a few suggestions.

If Baron Okura wants me for something worth-while that I could entrust to you for execution (I see from this work of yours that you could carry out anything I might design) I would be glad to come over to get it designed and started...Japan has a warm place deep in my heart.

But America is awakening to the importance of what I have done and is likely to keep me busy. Nevertheless, I think my charming little family would love a trip of three or four months, say, in the winter, to the country that has always fascinated me.

You and I might, together, do some fine things yet. If I were working with you again I could show you the tendencies to emphasize and those to avoid...in future. I've grown some myself. You are able to do great things, all you need is "pruning"and a little "more sand in the soil."

I think my hand is the hand to do the pruning...I who fed the branches too luxuriantly, perhaps. At any rate—my affection and loyalty all go over to you in best hope for the future.

Perhaps you and your family will come here again to prepare another great building for this new era in Japan—God knows Japan needs it...Who knows where or when it may happen?

November 23, 1930
Jacques André, Architect
Nancy, France

My dear Sir:

The material I have used for the molded blocks in the Millard Home and others is a simple mixture of Portland Cement Concrete—one of cement to four of sand.

The sand is rather coarse, sharp and clean. We like to vary the sand so the blocks will not be exactly alike. I use what is called the dry-mix that is just wet enough to take the shape of the hand and keep it when squeezed and this mixture is tamped into the molds by hand. It does not make a water-proof block used in this way, so we coat the inside of the block with asphalt when it is dry, and before setting the block in the wall.

The texture of the wet mixture is not so agreeable a surface but it would be more waterproof.

October 31, 1930
Raymond Hood
New York City, N.Y.

Dear Raymond:

Sitting in at the Tavern night before last with Andy Rebori and four or five others, a wisecrack attributed to me raised a laugh.

"Frank Wright says the Chicago Columbian Fair killed Architecture and the Chicago Fair in 1932 is going to bury it."

It is one of those stories "in character" that denial won't stop. I. K. Pond started the thing so far as I could learn. Of course I have said nothing at all about the Fair. Asked many times: "What about it?" My answer invariably is— "I know nothing at all about it."So far as I can see, it is exactly none of my damned business. So that if this quotation which seems to be going around pretty freely reaches you—you may know how much credit to give me.

(Undated) 1930
Raymond Hood
New York City, N.Y.

Dear Raymond:

Thanks for the stick—it was a lot of trouble to you or to somebody.

I want to say that your sense of humor, which is delightful, I was counting on when I wrote my last note to you—the only note, I guess, so far.

The witty-wrinkles at the corner of the eyes should be working in imagination when that note is read in-as-much as they can't work on paper.

I want nothing to embarrass our free relationship by any sense of anything else.

I am so glad to have found comradeship in my own profession at last—with you at the head of the procession.

Stand by me and don't let me spoil it by any "wise-cracks" or sarcastic suggestions. They are a habit of mine that I am trying to overcome.

My best to you—and Olgivanna wishes you all might spend a time with us all here in this most beautiful of country.

November 3, 1930
Mr. Jens Jensen
Ravinia, Illinois

Dear Jens:

Thanks for your note—just received, and the postcard from abroad. You must have had a bully time. We all hope you are well. You acknowledge Tallmage as a brother?

Sex jealousy though cruel is sometimes a noble passion but professional jealousy is never anything but cruel and mean. He has a bad case.

My work has suffered great hindrance in this country because of malicious propaganda by the "brother" architects themselves. God knows they should be my friends. But I have a different kind of success which they envy and would emulate, foolishly believing that to knock me boosts them in that direction.

However, even friends (like yourself for instance) seldom give me a hand unless dragged in by the beard or back-hair and intimidated? During 27 years for instance never has any work on your account come to me or any on my account gone to you, although I have had little or none to give these past ten years having been in deep trouble. It would be quite natural that you should want to work with me, whenever you could? yes? But is it that a Star is seldom willing to share with a Star. The Star will seek lesser men to accomplish his purpose, as a matter, he mistakenly thinks, of self-preservation. As a matter of fact I am "on my own" or I sink for this reason if for no other—and there are plenty of others, so far as professional give and take goes and I know it now. Time has run along far enough to show how the ground lies under my feet—I am resigned but not reconciled.

Our best to the Jensens.

November 27, 1930
Erich Mendelsohn
Berlin, Germany

My dear Erich Mendelsohn:

We still remember your visit to Taliesin with pleasure, and I have to thank you for your kindness to my son.

Some of your kind words concerning myself have reached me and I hope some of my good words for you have reached you—indirectly perhaps.

I am writing especially to ask your opinion concerning an exhibition of my work now going on in the United States. I am wondering if the German Society of Architects would sponsor the show and the German Government help them pay the expenses necessary and incidental thereto.

A young German working here with me is coming over to Germany in December and will call on you.

I hope you will come to Taliesin and bring Mrs. Mendelsohn—next Spring.

I should like some news concerning you—direct from yourself.

January 27, 1931
Mr. George H. Allen, Architect
New York City, N.Y.

My dear Mr. Allen:

Thank you for your kind suggestion. But I am afraid the truly distinguished company in which I should find myself would take me out of character into a situation so unusual as to be embarrassing.

I have no hobbies, belong to no clubs, have designed no projects and have no intimate side.

Mr. Murchison is an interesting writer and I am sure your series of articles will be a success. I shall myself read them, with pleasure.

February 3, 1931
Raymond Hood
New York City, N.Y.

My dear Ray Hood:

A situation I don't at all like is growing up around my "unemployment" in connection with the Chicago Fair. The disagreeable feature of the situation arises from the false assumption that the Fair is a public concern and representative of the country—which I'm sure from what you've said and what I've heard otherwise—is a mistake. It is not and is not intended to be. All I know directly about the situation is what you told me yourself. You said I was to do a building at the Fair, and later I made a suggestion in that connection to which you replied in a note concerned also with other matters, asking me to "leave it all to you." Of course, I have no other choice. It is not up to me in any way as I see it. As you gave me to understand it the present Architects got the Job direct from Dawes—and being pretty well satisfied with each other—feel it entirely within their rights to do the job themselves as they best can.

The private Nature of the enterprise not being generally understood—of course I've heard incessant complaints, accusations by the hundreds of injustice etc. etc.—and from all over the country. "The Nation" broke into print, more recently the "New Republic" but with no instigation from me. Now I'm asked to attend a public meeting on the subject to which the press is to be invited in New York in a couple of weeks.

I can't really see why the matter has been allowed to become so damned important either way—either by your committee or by my friends. But so it seems to be. Nor do I see that all this, once the Fair is confessed as a private enterprise, gets to you fellows in any way where you live. But until that is plain it does put me in an awkward situation, which I don't like at all, and which I propose to end in no uncertain terms at the proposed meeting.

Of course if the Fair aims to be representative of Modern Architecture the situation is too small and mean for a man like yourself. I don't know the others except as I met Walker and Corbett at the League dinner. I can only see and say that the Fair—being a private and personal affair made peculiar to yourselves by Dawes—I can see no reason why if you want to do it yourselves, since you got the drop of the hat, why you shouldn't run your race against time or whatever it is you choose to run against—and if you feel I would spoil your party—(it is noised around you do feel that way)—why that is your affair and they can figure it out. I am not interested. But if the Fair shows its face as Modern Architecture and is to be sold as such to the American Public in which I have a stake—equal at least to your own more recent one—in that connection—then only over my dead body, say I.

There has been some such attempt on Dr. Corbett's part in the past that got to me and raised the ruff on my neck some. But never mind until we get to that. What I want you to do, Ray, if you can, is to get permission to write me a letter in this connection that I can use at the meeting to put myself fairly and squarely where I belong and end the discussion once and for all. I don't know of anything in my career that has been so insulting to me as an Architect or to yourselves as well as the present impasse is becoming because of this misapprehension as to the Nature of the Fair as an enterprise.

I claim your friendship and you have mine but that doesn't make us eye to eye as Architects—as no one knows better than yourself.

(Undated) 1931
Pauline Schindler
Los Angeles, California

Dear Pauline:

I am glad to see you are set up for yourself on the Boulevard with a characteristic Schindler letter-head. It looks very nice; Rudolph is skillful. There is no reason whatever why not a series of Lectures by myself this Fall on the coast, if worth while. See what arrangements you can make—on a commission basis of course. And we will allow you to handle the exhibition when it reaches California.

If you intend showing any of my work in your exhibition I should like you to show to Lloyd all the photographs of the California work you take before you exhibit them. Also as the Architectural Record is getting out a book on my work this Summer I might like to use such as appealed to me as good, and the Record would pay for them now. So send me proofs. If you would be so good as to do this Pauline, I see no reason why Lloyd should "hang back." I am writing him, although I believe the young man has never had much faith in the loyalties of contemporary young architects.

And I myself have noticed this—that while many of my sworn adherents and generous admirers have in the past profited considerably by my work and by my own clients—I can remember no such instance ever happening to me concerning *them*.... It is a pity. But there is nothing to be done about it. I suppose I shall have to turn on them myself and show them up soon....

I think often of the little Los Angeles group. Lost to sight the past few years I have wondered how you yourself developed during these years of privation and struggle. I should sincerely love to see you all successful, but looking at the matter from an entirely selfish standpoint I do not see anything the group could do for me if they would or wanted to. I've seen, now, the performances of nearly fifty, and they are much the same in the end. There is no ambitious selfishness, it seems, like the selfish ambition of the artist architect. Sex-jealousy is far less subtle, deep, and destructive.

I have long been looking for something else, believing every so often I had found it only to see it go that characteristic way, eventually. I haven't cared much hitherto but I may be compelled to avoid it in future.

Meantime believe me.

Affectionately yours,

July 6, 1931
Mr. P. Belluschi
A. E. Doyle & Ass., Architects
Portland, Oregon

My dear Belluschi:

Your client is making a serious mistake looking toward the future. Only a vanishing present looks upon a "Georgian" outside as tolerable, now. He is subscribing to a lost cause.

Your sensible modern exterior has everything to commend it and, with the few alterations as to central feature I've taken the liberty to suggest, it would make a building creditable to your "donor." His Georgian design will only mark him as reactionary in an era when light was breaking all over the world.

I cannot see how any man at this time could wish to go into the record as false to his own posterity.

However, I know that donors will continue in the backwater a long time. I wish I might help. But taste is only personal idiosyncrasy, cultivated, and so has no logic but fear, no sense but sentimentality.

I think your plan simple and sensible and the exterior would mark an advance in culture for Portland.

Can't Doyle and Crowell stand up for Architecture?

January 19, 1932
Mr. Philip Johnson
Long Island City, New York

My dear Philip:

There is not much use in writing this letter. It will convince you of nothing except that I am hard to deal with and an uncompromising egotist as per propaganda and schedule.

All right. So be it. I shall at least have the luxury of living up to that part, such as it is, for which I am cast. I am going to step aside and let the procession go by with its band-wagon. I find I don't speak the same language nor am I in step with its aims and purposes. Architecture to me is something else.

If you had made the character of the show a little clearer to me in the beginning we might have saved some waste motion and expense, but I hope there is not much of that. By now money is so hard to find.

My telegram explains most of what I have to say.

I find myself rather a man without a country, architecturally speaking, at the present time. If I keep on working another five years, I shall be at home again, I feel sure.

But meantime the scramble of the propagandist "international" for the band-wagon must have taken place and the procession must be well on its way, without me.

It seems to me, I see too much at stake for me to countenance a hand-picked group of men in various stages of eclecticism by riding around the country with them, as though I approved of them and their work as modern, when I distinctly do not only disapprove but positively condemn them.

I respect Corbusier, admire van der Rohe, like Haesler, and many good men not in your show, if the list is as indicative as intended. Howe is respectable, and Lescaze, so far as I know, though a fledgling.

I could feel at home in a show including them, and such younger men as were earnestly at work trying to build noble and beautiful buildings, as I did when I was younger, and willing to patiently establish themselves as architects by that honest route—and claim success, step by step, as earned.

But I am sick and tired of the pretense of men who will elect a style, old or new, and get a building badly built by the help of some contractor and then publicize it as a notable achievement. This hits not one man only, but a type...

Propaganda is a vice in our country. High power salesmanship is a curse. I can at least mind my own business, if I can get any to mind, and not compete or consort with what are to me disreputable examples of disreputable methods that will get our future architecture nothing but an "international style." A cut paper style at that. I am aware of your sympathies in that direction, and of Russell's [Hitchcock]—and was prepared to respect both of you in it until I see the taint of propaganda in the personal examples you prefer.

I believe both of you sincere, but you are both beginning, and probably unaware of much that is too thin, too weak and too false in color not to fade.

But that is no reason why I should join your procession and belie my own principles both of architecture and conduct.

I am aware, too, of the ammunition this act of mine furnishes my enemies. Oh yes, I have so many! No man more.

But my eye is on a goal better worth trying for, even if I am called in before I reach it. If I am, I shall at least not have sold out!

Believe me, Philip, I am sorry. Give my best to Russell Hitchcock and I expect to see you both here at Taliesin early next summer—with your wives. If you haven't got them now you will have them by then?

February 11, 1932
Mr. Philip Johnson
New York City, N.Y.

Dear Philip:

The article on the show in the N. Y. Times was the silliest exposition I've seen of the "hide and horns." Such unbelievably childish statements and examples can only harm instead of help the cause of an architecture. The statements expressed there are indicative.

Why, I ask you, should I who have dedicated my lifetime to an ideal of organic architecture trail along with this attempt to steal the hide and horns of that ideal and make the animal come alive by beating the tom-tom?

I not only feel out of character but out of sympathy with the whole endeavor. I belie my whole cause by coming with you as I suspected I would when, suspiciously, I first withdrew. Now my worst suspicions are wholly confirmed.

It was only out of a desire to help your effort along that I consented to come in the first place. And now that I learn I am there, not that I longer count, but because I am historical; well, I am not hysterical but smiling a somewhat sarcastic smile.

The shameless and selfish essence of such promotion and propaganda as is back of this attitude is, in its essence, a fitting attribute of the exploit. And while I am by no means sure Oud and Rohe would approve (of course Corbusier would as he is the soul of your propaganda) it is of no consequence. It would be unfair to travel with you feeling as I do. I know now where I stand.

And I feel much better to have the enemies of an organic architecture where they belong—out in front. My wishes in this connection are final. I insist that every trace of my name in connection with your promotion be removed when the show at the Museum of Modern Art closes.

As you may imagine it is with difficulty and chagrin that I re-discover to what extent my devotion to principle in a great cause is valuable to my contemporaries. They compete and do not complete. But I should not complain. I have devoted myself to architecture for no other reason than my love for it. I should at least like to concede as much to them.

Perhaps with enough perspective I can.

I agreed to stay only for the New York show as I wired Lewis. [Mumford]. In fact I learned of the proposed tour only from the newspapers.

Be a good sport, Philip, and help me out as gracefully as possible.

February 15, 1932
Mr. Werner Moser
Zurich, Switzerland

My dear Werner:

Thank you for the "Werk." I am quite delighted by your little houses. The plans are good and you seem, in spite of an international list, to have advanced some individuality of your own. In fact there is some flavor of the "Swiss" that is refreshing. Your natural tendency would be toward the lean and hard and these buildings are, naturally, a little stiff—not quite free in proportion; still openings cut in the wall surfaces and a few stilts.

But the balconies with their iron work and awnings are yours—and so light and graceful and genuine. Your ironwork has not only point but imagination, a thing not seen in the international at all. I hope to see more use of such imagination in the building form itself.

Do not be afraid. Respect no formula. Live your own life surely as soon as you feel the ground under your feet. Every time I see the international chair I feel like I do when I see the Derby hat. It is a good chair but sterilizes any individual character in an exterior and classifies it right away. Let those make such a surrender who can do no better. I see you can do better. And I am encouraged.

We are pretty well here, though poorer and poorer in pocket. But we are happy and looking up and forward. "An Autobiography" comes out soon. That may change our outlook financially.

Give my love to one of the world's finest women—I mean Sylva, and your admirable father. He is a pretty good architect, you know, and you owe him much.

We all send love to you all—

(Undated) 1932
Mr. George Howe
Howe and Lescaze, Architects
Philadelphia, Pa.

Dear George:

(If you can take the liberty of calling me God I can take the liberty of calling you George?)

When I said "I wish I had him for a partner" I was envying Lescaze his promoter and defender. I get that way sometimes in my single-handedness but know that nature cut me out from all that when she made me. I would only make a partner's life miserable and he make mine—in all but riches—futile because I couldn't stand it to see him frustrated alongside. So that is that.

I am doing a little piece on "the designing partner" for fun. I suppose no-one will publish it, but it sems to me he is a bit on the shady side of pretense as he promotes himself just now.

It is hard to be understood.

I make a distinction between interior and exterior discipline—that is my whole case.

How to set up the one in line with the ideal as against the other in line with the expedient is the whole business of democracy as I see it. I agree entirely with your second diagnosis concerning our wretched abuse of liberty and lack of restraint. Democracy is communal individuality. We exaggerate personality and forget the communal. Never mind. Out of "too much" comes knowledge of what is enough.

No, the creative fire is here or nowhere. And culture is beginning out of chaos. The plant first, and the plant is a reached out civilization—then "cultivation" or culture. I think you use the word culture as the Germans use the word Kultur. To me words are not the same thing. Nature made the larkspur but culture made the delphinium. The physical body first: a civilization. Cultivation: then culture. But I may give the thing my own special significance.

At any rate, as you say, we have so much more in common than the old licentious order of taste that we should stand together and fight.

I find myself out in no man's land now, shot at from in front, ambushed on both flanks and shot at from the rear. How glad I should be of an honest—though free to differ—alliance. Some time I hope we meet and hold this valuable ground under our feet. The International, as presented, is the Geist der Kleinichkeit. Beethoven saw it in music and fought it as I see it in architecture today and fight it as I best damn can.

February 18, 1932
Mr. George Howe
Howe and Lescaze, Architects
Philadelphia, Pa.

Dear George Howe:

To get back to the "Green Pastures" and going on with the Moses figure: when Moses took the ten commandments from God himself he gave the commandments to his people as they were.

God did not tell Moses to imply or pretend that he, Moses, made them.

Now, if Moses had the creative ability of God he might have thrown the commandments away and made new ones on his own for the salvation of the people. But he seems to have been perfectly satisfied to leave them as they were from whence they came and got his people out of the wilderness.

But if Moses, being Moses, were merely ambitious to be God he would have taken the commandments and a la Gertrude Stein say he could change "thou shalt not steal" to read, say, "steal not shalt thou" or "shalt not thou steal" or "thou steal not shalt" etc. etc. ad nauseam, ad libitum with all ten.

Thus he might write a whole book and beat God easy enough proclaiming himself creator of a new creed for a better and more useful life for the people of the Earth, but never have gotten his people out of the wilderness.

Imagine God in these latter circumstances? Such treachery would disappoint him, and being only God would probably anger him. I am afraid Moses would get a swipe, somehow, in order to bring him to his senses. And then God, being only God, would give him another chance to get up and try again.

My dear George: your comparison was one step too low. This will sound vulgar but you started it....Frank Lloyd Wright is God in this matter and the International seeks to be Moses.

And the internationalist does what Moses might have tried to do a la Gertrude Stein. Invents formula, retouches already good designs, emphasizes the hollow places a little and scrapes it off a little and opens it out a little more, hardens it up some and they call the result a style—a "health house" too, I believe they call it? They even call it architecture.

Does this Frank Lloyd Wright like this spoiling of the sense? Would you like it, George? Perhaps you would. But if F.Ll.W. cares at all for the ideal he has no choice but to give it a blow between the eyes or a kick in the rump, well placed, to try to bring the thing to its senses and keep opportunity open for others and for himself. He is not dead yet....

Sincerely if ungraciously, I would like to be your friend if you needed one,

August 30, 1932
Mr. Eliel Saarinen
Director, Cranbrook School
Birmingham, Michigan

My dear Saarinen:

Would you write to me such a letter concerning the Fellowship that I might show it to people who could help with the buildings and industrial equipment of the School?

If these people felt that ten worth while architects thoroughly approved and would like to see them help it might smooth our way a little, because I imagine many material men and manufacturers fear that were they to commit themselves to a radical architect's venture like this they might antagonize the "field" and refuse.

I am sending a request similar to this to the ten architects I consider leaders whom the others follow.

Needless to say I should deeply appreciate a candid expression from you in any event.

[This request, for support from fellow architects regarding the merits of his proposed "school" or Fellowship, provides insight into which architects Mr. Wright found most congenial at that time. The architects he sent copies of this letter to, besides Saarinen, were George Howe, William Lescaze, John A. Holabird, John Wellborn Root, Ely Kahn, Thomas Lamb, Buckminster Fuller, Albert Kahn, and Joseph Urban.]

July 6, 1936
Aisaku Hayashi
Tokyo, Japan

My dear Aisaku:

No monument to the enlightenment of any race has ever stood up very long in the flesh. But the ideas and ideals it stood up for were started on their way and go on working.

Japan has no civilization now. She threw hers away to borrow one and henceforth can never be more than number two anywhere. She is the monkey nation among the other nation-animals. At her worst she is the baboon. So what is more natural in the circumstances than that she should mimic the worst antics of the culture she adopted: go further with the faults she mistakes for virtues?

And Okura. What is he? A nouveau riche with no deep feeling for the traditions of his race. Essentially a shallow pretentious opportunist. Aiding him, probably, there is some starved Building Company propaganda urging him to make up his mind in order to whitewash the Mitsiu ten-story buildings in Japan by building one more of them on the site of the distiguished new Imperial Hotel. All Tokyo, so say the more intelligent travelers who return from there, is becoming just one extensive modern garage. All sensibility, all of the characteristic fruits of a genuine Japanese culture, have been destroyed by this monkeyfied young Japan.

The Imperial took off its hat to that genuine Japanese culture and tried to show how the new might be true to the old and how the new might be better for the old. It was the only place in modern Tokyo where one might gather—in modern terms—some sense of honor for what Japan was.

Now it all has to go into the pot to make a monkey-feast for a day. Just as the thought of the Western world is turning away from tall buildings toward general decentralization her foolish imitator goes on with what her pattern is already learning to throw away.

Well, Aisaku, such is imitation and its consequences always. But this must be the worst case anywhere on record, I think. When Tokyo slaps her Imperial Hotel in the face to run after tall building profits (or prophets) she is the monkey not the man and is sure to lose, straight away, what little prestige she had left among the nations she imitates. Who will want to go to Japan to occupy a tall office building hotel just like any other in any town around the world? Why try to beat mediocrity at its own game? And who will respect her destruction of a thought-built edifice memorializing her own better self?

None, of course.

But that will make not much difference to the generation and circumstance to which Okura (the rich man's son) belongs. You would think some reverence for his father might hold his ambition's greed in check if nothing else? Or would you think so?

Let the Imperial go then. The thought it represents it will stand up for. And no martyrdom of the superior by the inferior ever hurt the great cause of the advancement of mankind even where buildings were concerned.

The money makers are more clearly seen everyday as busy monkeyfiers. So, for one, I decline to worry. When the time comes we will hold a ceremony to celebrate the cause which the destruction of your Japanese memorial can only serve to push forward. Let Okura lie where he will fall.

His ten story mediocrity which betrays his People will come down in its turn. It will soon come down because standing up it is destructive of everything a noble civilization must stand for. It could better serve it lying there a wreck.

I shall not lift a finger to save the Imperial Hotel. It is dedicated to a noble Japan I have loved and have learned much from.

If an inferior Japan, a Japan that not only I but the whole race of mankind is learning, now, to despise, should turn upon it and prefer the vile gods of trade to the ancestral gods that once lived in their civilization—why should I mourn except for the death of a unique people?

The new Imperial Hotel is not mine. It belongs only to those who understand what it meant and appreciate what it stood for and know why it stood there. They are increasingly more but they are still few compared with the many who neither feel nor think.

The Okuras are as many as there are pieces of money in circulation. The sooner they have their way the sooner they are out of the way, and a fairer nobler world will be on the way.

Faithfully—Aisaku—yours as always with love to the faithful Endo,

[Hayashi was a member of the committee that selected Mr. Wright to design the Imperial Hotel. He was also its manager.]

November 7, 1936
Mr. Arthur Peabody
State Architect, Madison, Wisconsin

My dear Arthur Peabody:

You mention this matter of an "oral examination" before I can be allowed to be an architect in my home state.

Certainly I am willing to be tried but ask that I—like any another man before me in a similar position—be tried by my peers and not by officials who may hold their office by way of theory not practice or because of some political preferment. I also ask that the hearing be open to whoever wants to be there and that a complete and accurate stenographic record be kept of the proceedings in every detail by two competent stenographers—one to be appointed by myself and another by my judge. I am to have a copy to use as I see fit.

Meantime my client, who wants to build and who will pay for the building in the design of which he has come to me for assistance, is subject to delay.

Is it fair that he be tried also for coming to me for assistance? Is it judicious that his interests be further injured by officious interference?

Perhaps some way can be found to allow him to make preparations at least for his building while his choice of an architect is being passed upon by his own state.

All of which raises the question (I think it is time to raise it) as to the wisdom of such punctilio as these rules and regulations to interfere with him and with me in the circumstances: rules that have only served to create a harbor of refuge for the inexperienced and the theoretically expert but practically incompetent. We need fewer rules and wiser regulations.

I believe that the so-called "license" laws for architects as they now stand are detrimental to the future of organic architecture. I have seen that they protect the weak and ignore or disqualify the strong by way of mere technicalities having no real bearing upon nor any direct relation to the merits in any case or proving the fitness of any man to be entrusted to building buildings for his people. I believe the sentiment of the more able members of my profession is turning against them.

I welcome an opportunity to present this view of the case.

How far must I journey and how long must I wait for this opportunity?

And (incidentally) I would like to know who my judges will be?

SEPTEMBER 8, 1937
FRANK LLOYD WRIGHT
TALIESIN, SPRING GREEN, WISCONSIN

AM IN CHICAGO FOR TOMORROW ONLY. WOULD LIKE VERY MUCH TO DRIVE TO TALIESIN AND PAY MY RESPECTS IF CONVENIENT TO YOU. YOUR TELEPHONE REPORTED OUT OF ORDER. PLEASE WIRE REPLY BLACKSTONE HOTEL, CHICAGO.

LUDWIG MIES VAN DER ROHE

[When Mies van der Rohe first came to visit Taliesin to pay his respects to Mr. Wright, whom he devotedly called "My Master," he was

escorted by an American architect who spoke fluent German. Mies spoke only a little English, and during the tour of Taliesin conducted by Mr. Wright, Mies' companion insisted on translating all that Mr. Wright was saying. In the course of the tour around the buildings, the American kept making snide comments in German on the various small faults in construction (much of Taliesin had been built or remodeled by apprentices learning about construction by actually doing it). "Look at the detail," he would say. "See how the wood mitre has opened up. Isn't that dreadful?" His remarks continued for some time until Mies turned to him with a fiery look in his eye and said: "Shut up! Can't you see that you are in the presence of great architecture?"]

March 28, 1939
Mr. Frank Lloyd Wright
Scottsdale, Arizona

My dear Mr. Wright:

A few days ago I arrived in this country and shall be staying here for about two months. Naturally my most earnest desire is that I might meet you personally. My short visit last autumn afforded no opportunity for a trip to Wisconsin, and for that reason I did not write you at that time.

My wife and I expect to make a round trip of your various buildings, and I am looking forward with keen anticipation to meeting you at the very first opportunity. I am told here by friends that you are going to Europe this spring, but I sincerely hope that before you leave America I may have the privilege of a short visit with you. It may be difficult for me to travel to Arizona as my little job at the World's Fair will keep me tied here in New York for some weeks to come. However, in no event should I like to miss an opportunity to contact personally the only architect in the world whom I have truly admired. I feel that contact with you would prove of immense personal value to me.

I most sincerely hope it may be possible to arrange a meeting with you.

Cordially yours,
Aalto

April 3, 1939
Mr. Alvar Aalto
New York City, N.Y.

My dear Alvar Aalto:

You will be most welcome at Taliesin in Wisconsin with Mrs. Aalto of course. We are sailing for England on the Queen Mary April 21st—but will be Taliesin April 16th and would be happy to have you spend a few days with us in the country.

I sincerely hope you can come.

July 17, 1939
Mr. Kenneth Bayes, Royal Institute of British Architects
London, England

My dear Kenneth Bayes:

The ancient East and the awakening West do meet upon ground common to both. I went to Japan sympathetic to interpret her own philosophy in terms of modern (Western) building. The Imperial Hotel is such interpretation. But the buildings preceding that (and there were many) had no such purpose because I knew little or nothing of the East until 1906 when I first went to Japan. I saw then and see now nothing inconsistent in their form of nature worship and the form I felt as my own before I knew of theirs.

No. Gurdjieff has had no influence whatever upon me or my work. I met him only several years ago through my present wife who was a pupil of his. We met some fourteen years ago. There was much in common however between his philosophy and my own practices which I recognize as proof of the universal validity of both.

As for Ouspenski, I think the spiritual interpretation of the simple three dimensions we have familiarized is all we need to be able to use infinite dimensions, so I've taken very little interest in him. Gurdjieff seems to me to be his master—so far as he goes.

I derive most collateral support from the Chinese LaoTze. I recommend him to you. But acquaintance with his philosophy came to me late in my life after the ideals and philosophy of an organic architecture were firmly established by my own practice of them. So, in him, I found again not so much inspiration as confirmation.

My old master, Louis Sullivan, knew none of them and yet the ground-work of an organic architecture was in his mind when he died.

So the pigeonholes became less significant as Time goes along—the vision of the whole more important. It is more important to feel and act in harmony with one's sense of the whole than to classify.

If you come this way, come to see us at work at Taliesin. I sympathize with your aims.

January 20, 1943
Architects Alabyan and Arkin
Moscow, Russia

My dear Alabyan and my dear Arkin:

We have read your brotherly letters with appreciation and affection. Our hearts went out to you long ago in this horrible human conflagra-tion. We feel we have done so little and are enraged that our country was so late in realizing your strength and importance. First of all we should have come to aid Russia's victory.

We do not see that what both you and we love most and are best able to work for is going to be so much benefited by any *military* victory, because force has never organized anything. But when one's own home-land is affected and violence is done to all we hold sacred and love with all our hearts it is hard, if not inhuman, to think of right and wrong. Or even to think at all. We only feel and hate and strike—to kill.

But the world's creative artists see that a Monstrosity is let loose upon the lives of the whole of mankind by selfish groups of men who got con-trol of it before they could control themselves. The whole is now out of hand and turning to destroy the economic-royalists who selfishly used it to enrich themselves. If you and I who belong to the creative artists and thinkers of this world do not help to check this wild force now and turn it back where it belongs to be used for the peace and happiness of the peoples of the world I think Western Civilization is doomed. Even before peace comes that is our pressing problem in the Western World. It may be too late after victory is won. Things go back then, not forward.

I have always regarded Russia as the connecting link between the East and West.

As Russia turns East or West so will the future of this world be settled. Now that sea-lanes are no longer lanes of shameful aggression and brutal conquest, Central Asia, this time under Russian leadership, may again become the pivot of the Modern World as it used to be the center of the Ancient World.

The plane has changed everything and chemistry is changing everything still further.

I well remember the celebration in Moscow of the Russian aviators' first flight over the pole to America. What a big time that was and how it thrilled us all.

It was more significant I think than we realized then. As a matter of fact all frontiers are much less important now. Nationalism is fading since it became the enemy of all Nations. The back doors of Nations are now front doors and all the doors are soon of little or no consequence. The trade and racial barriers must come down—actually. But it will take a whole generation to realize these things. Stupid war goes on just as though we were back in horse-and-buggy days. Men on foot are fed into mechanized forces as we feed straw into a threshing machine, but in the case of men they are fed into machines not only without mercy but without much effect on the whole. Hoping for victory is a vain hope unless Russia wins.

Then, Central Asia may become again the great world center! And since the old time carriers of Transportation are gone or going so fast it does not seem so greatly important where Russia's western frontier lies—if she gets it entirely clear of all small jealous nations and defines it once and for all where Moscow, Leningrad and the Caucasus are safe for her and she gets her own people back.

I have felt that Russia and a free India, a free China, later on joined perhaps by a chastened Japan would be the growing power and the grouping that would restore the balance of the world—with the U.S.A. as good friend and neighbor across the Pole. All forms of Empire are dead. I don't mean this for a "balance of power" because I believe that is all dead hereafter, so much as a measure for development profiting by the mistakes of the West.

The Moslem would be a natural ally of that friendly group and eventually the African races would be also.

If our emancipation from the money power despotism that drives the West to madness does not come out of this World-war the West is doomed. The profit-motive has made Western civilization powerful and hard to convince. It may take another war to do it.

We often think of you and our Moscow friends, your good wives, Colle and his wife, Nikolsky and his wife, and the Vesnin brothers, Yofan and his wife too.

I tried to see you, Alabyan, when you were in New York but I was there for only a few days and don't know if you got my several messages because no answer came. I wrote Yofan a note when he was there but got no reply.

You may imagine our concern for you all. We could not bear to hear that Suchanov is destroyed. And while we feel that most of Moscow could be much better built by you, all if it were destroyed, we could not bear to think of the old Russian Landmarks gone forever. There is so much in common between your land and our land. Not only the flowers, the weeds, the trees and rivers, the landscape—even the weather—but our own hearts and minds. I have always felt at home with the Russians. It is a natural liking I have for them and feel it is lucky that Olgivanna speaks Russian and grew up in your Caucasus. We could not bear to think of that land as German and of course it never will be. India also claims deep anxiety and sympathy at this time. Russia is her natural brother and must lead her out of bondage. She has been dormant long enough and with proper leadership she can emerge into a great spiritual World power.

We still show Russian films in our little cinema at Taliesin. We have seen about seventy or eighty of your best ones, so far as we know them. There is an artistry about them and a vitality in them not matched by any other films. I glory in the Russian spirit.

It would be pleasant if we could all walk and talk together at Taliesin as we did at Suchanov and perhaps we will. Work has ceased for us and we are doing only what we can do to keep Taliesin together for post-war work and Freedom. And to preserve social sanity.

Meantime, be assured of our love and best hope. We wish we could send you great shiploads of your heart's desire. There is still plenty of everything in the country it seems but hard to get it over there. It should go across the Pole.

Please remember us to all our Moscow friends and fire a salute to your own Stalin in our name.

March 1, 1943
Jens Jensen
Ravinia, Illinois

Dear Jens:

You dear old Prima Donna—I don't know whether you exaggerate your own sense of yourself or exaggerate my sense of myself. It doesn't much matter either way. But I think you would be interested to see how a minority report, such as I might bring in with my experience in the study of structural Form as interpretation of nature, would compare with yours, you who imitate nature.

Yes, our points of view diverge. But that wouldn't prevent me from helping you get a job you wanted to do. You are a realistic landscapist. I am an abstractionist seeking the pattern behind the realism—the interior structure instead of the comparatively superficial exterior effects you delight in. In other words I am a builder. You are an effectivist using nature's objects to make your effects.

The matter is unimportant except that I should think a man like you who has lived as long as you have (in times past cribbing some of my "patterns" to decorate your pictures) would be curious so see what the other fellow's view-point could reach. I find that I can be interested in that with which I supremely disagree, and I continually learn from my opposites.

This is not to ask you to sign my appeal for a job to help make the world a better world to live in but to sympathize with a man to whom age has not brought tolerance and vision but instead animus and opinion—which he values above discovery and friendship.

As always,

November 15, 1944
Mies van der Rohe
Chicago, Illinois

Dear Mies;

We are celebrating Thankgiving on Thursday, November 30th. We are looking forward to having you with us—

Sincerely,

September 25, 1945
Mr. Frank Lloyd Wright
Taliesin, Spring Green, Wisconsin

Dear Mr. Wright:

I have delayed writing you to thank you for the wonderful weekend at Taliesin because I have been trying to locate the Beethoven Quartet Op. 135 that I promised to send you.

I hope you like it as much as I do. It seems to me to represent, among Beethoven's works, the same height of achievement that you have now reached with the Museum and with the Loeb house.

As I mentioned to you, the Museum of Modern Art wishes to do something about improving the quality of war memorials. Naturally, the first name that occurs to us is yours. A design by your hand, we feel, if widely enough broadcast throughout the country would do more to point the way to some American solution of an American problem than anything else we can imagine. I am aware of your feelings about towns and villages, and naturally agree with them. We are, however, faced by the immediate problem of designing symbols for war remembrance in the towns which always exist. We need your help in imagining what could be a proper symbol.

I do not wish to ask lesser artists for ideas on memorials until I have heard from you either accepting or refusing our request.

Yours affectionately,
Philip C. Johnson

October 3, 1945
Philip C. Johnson
The Museum of Modern Art
New York City, N.Y.

Dear Phil:

I do not believe in monuments.

Memorials are better if they are useful to those who live in the memories they memorialize. So memorial for what? Where? When?

Symbols are out.

Let's face the modern reality—true romanticism.

Sincerely,

September 28, 1946
Aisaku Hayashi
Tokyo, Japan

Dear Aisaku:

As you may imagine to hear from you again is better than good. I've had you and Endo San and our other Japanese boys in mind meantime this murderous world chamber of horrors. I would like to see you all again.

Japan meant so much to me and was so good to me—I can never forget.

I wish there was something I could do [*regarding postwar city planning in Japan*] but political influence in our country is beneath contempt. I have none and want none.

I would love to come to see Japan again because I am sure the heart of Nippon is still there where it grew, and wiser now may find the ways and means that belong to it as a true culture of the human spirit.

When this upsurge of all that is evil in human kind dies down again I hope to come over to the land I loved next to my own.

Give my love to Takake and the boys. If you get over here come and stay with me—

October 21, 1947
H. Th. Widjeveld
Oosterbeek, Holland

My dear Widjeveld:

You are one of the occasions that weigh on my conscience. I have not known just how to square myself with myself where you are concerned so not knowing what to write I did not write.

But your frank request to come to the U.S.A. and join me deserves a frank answer.

You were right when, faced with a part in my enterprise (was it more than twenty years ago?) you said, "He is difficult to work with. It will take many years to build up this place. I have only ten thousand dollars. I do not know what to do." That was well said.

Since then many years have passed. I have earned and spent probably a half million on this place and Arizona and all is yet unfinished. But, of course, much has been done since you saw it. We keep on as a "Foundation" now, tax exempt.

You were right in your conclusion that I would be difficult to work with. In fact I am impossible to work with...by any but one trained in and accustomed for many years to my way of work, that is to say. My disposition is that of a solo creative worker—even now as you must know. So what outcome for a man of your wide attainments and boundless ambition but almost no experience in my way of work and life with me except one of frustration and eventual ill will?

Two rams in one small sheep pasture are certainly one too many. I would like to be of help to you and yours—your appreciation reached me when my fortunes were at low ebb and I am not ungrateful at this distance.

But what shall it be? What would work out best for you in our country over here—I do not know.

This country is over-filled with left wing modernists of whom you are one. There is Gropius, Corbu, Mies, Mendelsohn, Breuer, and others. They are still there with the negation I made in 1906 and the emphasis of the horizontal I practiced in 1910.

To add another advocate of this "reaction" would not square with my creative conscience. Were you to go deeper than they and be able to controvert the cliched superficial aesthetic they now stand for, your advent on this side might be propitious and a chair in some university a blessing all around. You seem to me when you talk a man of deeper feeling and greater vision than those men. But when you build I see much the same character of thing in what you do—therefore naturally in what you would teach.

The breach between myself and these men has widened. They think, speak and work in two dimensions while idealizing the third and vice versa. I feel that I am as far beyond them now as I was in 1910 and their apostasy has only served to betray the cause of an organic architecture in the nature of materials which I believe to be the architecture of Democracy.

The thing they do is to me distinctly Nazi. And they cannot so see it at all. Why swell their ranks with another advocate because you were an admirer of mine back there in the days when? The Universities are loaded with these imports and while I suppose it is all better than the country might have had without them, it is all a miscarriage of the deeper thing I desired and in which I believed and for which I hoped.

Yes, modern architecture, so called, is way back there in 1910 so far as its actual body now goes as the latest thing in education.

You are naturally an enthusiast with taste and skill, a boundless ambition and energy equal to it. So in what and where could Widjeveld find satisfaction—realization of himself?

Frankly I do not know unless in a teacher's berth somewhere over here, and I do not want to augment the present tangent trend by my friendship because I know no good ever came or will come of temporizing with one's "ideal" just to be kind to a friend or be on good terms with oneself.

So, dear man, what shall I do for you? I would love to have you visit us again—would invite you and your wife as a guest with pleasurable anticipation—would do what I might do to secure you satisfaction somewhere.

But you could not ("nor any older man I fear") *work with me.*

I am too far gone in place and time with my own technique to employ the technique of another. And my time is getting too short to think of doing so. Taliesin is not what you seem to think.

You deserve a berth of your own by now and all I could do would be to give you a little shovelful of coals and help you start a little hell of your own somewhere but, as I imagine, even that is, in the circumstances, rather late for you my dear Widjeveld?

Let's see...	Saarinen	
	Gropius	
	Breuer	
on the one	Mies	
hand...	Mendelsohn	Frank Lloyd Wright
	Chermayeff	
	Corbu (off and on)	
	Lescaze *et al.*	
	Now Widjeveld?	

After these come the heterogenous breed, increasing by way of the short cut and push and what have you? You have the present equivocal situation in Modern Architecture with which I am dissatisfied.

Now the personality involved does not prevent me from doing everything I can for you as a friend. That is something else and please tell me what in particular at this moment I can do best—

Sincerely—

October 25, 1947
Mies van der Rohe
Chicago, Illinois

My dear Mies:

Somebody has told me you were hurt by remarks of mine when I came to see your New York show. And I made them to you directly, I think. But did I tell you how fine I thought your handling of your material was?

I am conscious only of two "cracks." One: you know you have frequently said you believe in "doing next to nothing" all down the line. Well, when I saw the enormous blow ups the phrase, "Much ado about your 'next to nothing'" came spontaneously from me.

Then I said the Barcelona Pavilion was your best contribution to the original negation and you seemed to be still back there where I was then.

This is probably what hurt (coming from me), and I wish I had taken you aside to say it to you privately because it does seem to me that the whole thing called Modern Architecture has bogged down with the architects right there on that line. I didn't want to classify you with them—but the show struck me sharply as reactionary in that sense. I am fighting hard against it myself.

But this note is to say that I wouldn't want to hurt your feelings—even with the truth. You are the best of them all as an artist and a man.

You came to see me but once, and that was before you spoke English many years ago. You never came since, though often invited.

So I had no chance to see or say what I said then and say now.

Why don't you come up sometime—unless the break is irreparable—and let's argue.

                                   Affection,

March 7, 1949
Philip C. Johnson
New York City, N.Y.

Dear Phil,

Have just read a squib in The New Yorker concerned with your latest Museum exploitation. I wish you would write and tell me why the

museum prefers to present to the American people these very features
and phraseology of my own under the name of one Marcel Breuer—

Now count me out of anything in connection with your pastorate at
the Museum of Modern Art. Your proteges now have the seeds and
seem to imagine they can raise the flowers under names satisfactory to
yourself. Why try to climb on the bandwagon this dishonest way. A little
honest attitude and I would move over to give you and your foreign
legion a seat.

Sincerely,

January 2, 1950
Philip C. Johnson
New York City, N.Y..

Dear Phil:

Our relationship needs a house-cleaning—

January 6, 1950
Mr. Frank Lloyd Wright
Taliesin West, Scottsdale, Arizona

Dear Mr. Wright:

You are right. May I visit you?

I made a speech in your defense last night at the Architectural League
Meeting on War Memorials and was soundly booed for it. I guess we all
still have a fight on our hands.

As ever, your faithful admirer,
Philip

January 13, 1950
Mr. Philip C. Johnson
New York City, N.Y.

Dear Phil:

I don't like to have your gore on my hands in my own house. But if you are willing to shed it—choose your own time.

April 21, 1951
Philip C. Johnson
Museum of Modern Art, New York, N.Y.

My dear Phil:

Yes...you are a clever boy. You put me now where if I refuse your offer of a generous exhibition of the Johnson opus I deprive my clients (they sent me a check for $20,000.00 last Christmas as a mark of appreciation) of advertising invaluable to them.

As for myself, I have no wish to deprive my client of anything nor have I much taste myself for further "exhibition" though I see the possibilities of the single building show as you describe it, if carried out with resourceful intelligence. You should have that or be able to command it.

So the answer is Yes. If you qualify as you propose. I am sick of having you for an enemy anyway Phil. When someone you've liked much gets into that category the feeling is unwholesome. Several well intentioned people have recently warned me that you were no friend of mine. My answer was yes—so you are telling me. You once upon a time wrote me a note that warmed my heart toward you. The ambiguity of the letter and following events I ascribed to the ambiguity of your position—a practicing architect eligible for a job sitting in judgement upon his competitors in a public place. A hypocrite was bound to that issue, Philip. I guess you have thought it over and came to a decision on your own account. But that issue is dead enough in the present state of the profession of Architecture, where every move of practically every architect is worse and the whole tribe stinks when the lid is off. The loss of a friend is more and more serious to me as I grow up. I always deplored your loss....

Let's be friendly again.

Affection,

April 3, 1952
Mr. Frank Lloyd Wright
Taliesin West, Scottsdale, Arizona

Dear Mr. Wright:

My congratulations on the success of the Guggenheim Museum! Edgar [*Kaufmann*] and I have had long talks about how wonderful it would be to have that great building dominate our greatest avenue. The Museum of Modern Art would like very much to formalize our greeting to your museum by giving a one-building show to your design. Will there be a model and, if so, could we show the original design at the same time? It would be of the greatest interest to the public, and it seems to us that it would also help the Guggenheim Foundation to a good publicity send-off.

Devotedly,
Philip

January 10, 1953
Mr. Thomas H. Creighton, Editor
Progressive Architecture
New York City, N.Y.

Dear Creighton:

Thanks for the advance article by and on Vlassov. Myself, the honored guest of the Architects' Convention, Moscow 1937, I went over hoping to save the Soviet from the reaction from the so called Modern. But I encountered that thing of Jeanneret's (the Crow) utterly idiotic from every standpoint and I found myself too late to do much good. The reaction to that confirmed ignorance had set in. The Russians were mighty nice to me, but they had seen little of my work and knew less of my philosophy. To them I was a name. The Soviet Architecture in their work at the Paris and New York Fairs was indebted to my work but they were on the run.

In the main, of course, Vlassov is right enough and if you will read "Organic Architecture looks at Modern Architecture" published by the Architectural Record, May 1952, you will find my answer to Vlassov et al. But of course like their ideology, they have the cart before the horse. You might send it on to him.

His stand is based not upon American Organic Architecture about which he apparently knows nothing at all but upon the European invasion of that Architecture, imitations now a dime a dozen—in the West. Going East.

Just imagine (by looking at our own slate) how long the Soviet must work and wait to show anything worthy of modern materials, methods, or men—or their ideas.

My heart aches for them and I can't help—

June 12, 1953
Mr. Frank Lloyd Wright
Taliesin, Wisconsin

Dear Mr. Wright:

For some years I have been wanting to write to you. It seemed time now to thank you, to say, I too have been aware, through all this time, of what you have given to us all, the living form, the sense of spatial relationship and meaning, man stating himself in dignity and nobility, monumentally. My gratitude has expressed itself only to others, never to you.

You know what you are. Of our love you also, surely, know? Yet one wants to say it, directly to you.

May I come to you for an hour or two, somewhere, at Spring Green or Taliesin West, or wherever?

And now, a further matter to speak of.

RMS [Rudolph M. Schindler] is in hospital fatally ill, with little time left. (Does not know; wants no one to be aware he is ill; wants no word of sympathy.)

In this desperate moment, to hear from you would be the most beautiful thing—the longed for return, the paternal benediction, needed and unconsciously awaited, at the extreme moment. How painful the break between you, so many years ago, he never said; the pain was walled in total silence. You were always, for him, the central radiant source. He knew himself your son.

At the end, it is needful to complete all circles, resolve all opposites and unfulfilments. (RMS and I do not communicate. He knows nothing of this letter to you. Our son, the frail Mark, has in the last week become a father, a cause for joy.)

According to report, you continue in timeless and flourishing creativity. Your students tell me that there is *no* possible architectural idea which is not already stored away in your blueprint drawers.

You have found the forms of verity. And truth, like courage, is contagious.

If you write, let it be, please, very soon.

> In gratitude, loyalty, and love,
> Pauline [*Pauline G. Schindler*]

June 12, 1953
Rudolph M. Schindler
Los Angeles, California

Dear Rudolph:

Somebody—must have been Pauline—told me you are hospitalized.

No matter how ambition may lead us astray, the old bonds still hold and I am sorry my once faithful helper should suffer. My best feelings go to you to tell you I still cherish memories of your ready smile and vivacious wit. Your talents served me well amid those of a lot of liars and pretenders whose success is ephemeral—worthless to humanity.

So Rudolph, dear man—here's to you in your extremity. If I can help you in any way let me know.

> Affection,

Critic Grant Manson wrote an article for the Architectural Review entitled "Wright in the Nursery," dealing with the Froebel Kindergarten education that Mr. Wright received from his mother. Mr. Wright wrote the following response:

June 18, 1953
Grant Manson
Sioux City, Iowa

My dear Grant Manson:

The Editors of the Architectural Review have just sent me a copy containing a leading article by you, "Wright in the Nursery," which fascinates and pleases me because somehow you did get to the source of my mother's contact with Froebel, which I never really knew, and you are perfectly right regarding the formative power and direction the "kindergarten" gave my instincts and could beyond all else give children if properly applied.

But the direct comparisons of Froebelian color-pattern and plan-forms with ultimate buildings is—while extremely ingenious—only a haphazard guess and might go backward as well as forward. In any posterior view or estimate it is well to take this into account, always.

The early influences may have opened the mind of youth to the same sources of inspiration that Froebel himself or other elemental minds and forces may have received. As for instance the article by Professor Tselos of Minnesota U. which I send with my comments.

I have of late had occasion to read many gazings into the crystal ball to see whence came the image. Many seem to be cutting out the head of the drum to find whence comes the sound, but I especially value your contribution. It is nearer true than any of the others.

July 8, 1953
Perry Prentice, Editor
Architectural Forum, New York City, N.Y.

My dear Perry:

You are entirely a reasonable man, but you are on a special spot. It would be difficult to show you from where you sit what is above and beyond reason—that is to say, where inspired architecture begins or ends. I can't hope to do so except indicate what should be evident by a little first-aid to enlightened attention. All the so-called "International Style" really represents is a facade derived from my own work. And yet it is made to seem to be contributed by "prominent names" serving American Architecture since 1921. You begin there when you "include us all in."

The streamlined effects contributed by my work, to Germany, by Wasmuth Publication in 1910 (ten years or more after they were originated and practiced) were then and are now the true basis of every single feature the Bauhaus or leCorbusier have since practiced *as though original with themselves*. Easy to prove this if worthwhile. *Is it worthwhile?* I wonder?

This truth has become camouflaged and confused by the Museum of Modern Art together with a group of apostates glad to see ideas come from abroad rather than from "at home." Some of these are now your editors, and subscribers too, to a considerable extent. So you are not likely to be educated in American Architecture prior to 1921 by them—even if they knew enough about it themselves, which is doubtful to me.

To now understand what happened by looking back over the outside of the thing (judging by *names*) would require the sort of first hand, direct view I myself possess: having seen it all come in from here and there—little by little—and be renamed each time as occasion arose. This affair has gone on since 1921. No protest meantime.

But there is still plenty of evidence aboveboard abroad and plenty here at home to really insure no fear of any dislocation of truth in the long run. Truth has a strange way of coming up and coming back. There are men like Lewis Mumford, Bruno Zevi, Giancarlo di Carlo, Talbot Hamlin, Ralph Walker, etc., etc., etc., who have already put the truth of the affair on record. But, not even then has the nature of the principle involved been made clear. This is my shame now as the tide of mediocrity rises.

You see, when any original impulse begins to be taken for a ride because of its mere *effects* (in this case streamlining by way of steel and glass) and a splurge of new names comes along to take that ride, you have the sort of thing you now see in so-called "Modern Architecture" spread wide as the "International Style" by promoting influences like museums and magazines.

Now I feel not only entitled but *obliged* to show the abuse of the ideas which I consider to be the *original of American Architecture*, because the deeper philosophy behind that countenance is being neglected in order to produce a fashionable *futility* being taught as the real thing when it is merely another superficial *facility*. Architecture today is, first of all, in need of a sound philosophy upon which to base a new aesthetic. Nature-study is its only source. Organic Architecture is, to date, its only fruit.

Architects can't get the needed *philosophy* from esthetes (most of them perverted scientists or scientific perverts or commercial opportunists. Anyhow, *no esthetes can ever produce the philosophy we need now.*

The Philosophy of Organic Architecture is anti-Greek, but its "effects" have been made over into a fashion by such "aesthetes" as function in the pansy-bed at and around the Museum of Modern Art. Some little good has come of it, no doubt. But *more harm than good.* Eventually ruin. Even now we see the degradation if we look straight. Those who squirm or swim in the "new facility" meantime are all beneficiaries of this travesty. So they imagine.

But the great original ideas suffer because of this incestuous parasitism. To me "LeCorb" is a brash parasite. "Mies" is a pitiful survival of Greek parasitism. Gropius is distinctly not so much a parasite as a pervert from Architecture to Science "apropos" of our national deterioration. By way of his teaching the confusion grows as to whether Architecture is to be an Art or become a Science in America.

As standardization goes it is expedient, certainly, to teach Architecture expendable as a Science and best served by the appropriate and inevitable cliche you are all exploiting now whether you know it or not. As editor, Perry, this may be all right too. You are not primarily concerned with the life or death of a great ideal of a great Art.

I am.

I think you are all right in many of the exceptions you take to my way of defending the great ideas to which I have given my life without stint or any compromise worth mentioning. When I revolted on paper several weeks before the H. B. [House Beautiful] explosion, knowing nothing whatever of it, and sent the revulsion to you: you denied me a voice in what you call the FORUM, because I was impolitic.

That was right enough too. No, believe me: if I saw the real thing in architecture—the organic thing—coming out of all this rush for a seat in the wagon I have myself driven thirty eight years before your 1921 I would not try to do anything more than praise, as I might.

But I see that cherished "cause" betrayed by stupid or scheming impulses and exploited by conscienceless names, at home and abroad, with no understanding or feeling for what they selfishly destroy.

Now, how can you see all this from where you have, only so lately, been sitting? It is more or less ancient history and is probably being deliberately obliterated for another decade at least by everyone you know. Certainly editorial policy is salesmanship.

As a matter of fact, Perry, I guess I have lived too long—long enough, that is, to witness what usually takes place after a man's death— both plus and minus. If I take the plus the minus comes too? The thing is loaded, either way.

Affection,

As a matter of fact also, Perry, to "include everybody in," what I really was had to be "included out."

So, if an original like myself is to be "internationalized" I must be de-individualized. See? Of course the process is not pleasing to the original who has lived too long and it is not at all enhancing to *quality*. All History readily shows this. Society always gets the desired *quantity* but gets it at expense to *quality*. That's all. That is where we are right now in this quest of *A* style. I am kicking because quantity is what lives on while quality must die. I would give and take— QUALITY for mine.

Now, as things could be internationalized, Perry, what I once represented and upheld with all my love of Life can no longer go far beyond an *average* level. What I wrote and the H. B. was rash enough to print, *if you will read it again*, should make this clear enough?

I never did believe in artificial insemination.

September 28, 1953
Frank Lloyd Wright
Taliesin, Wisconsin

Dear Mr. Wright:

Your letter to R.M.S., so quickly and blessedly sent in response to mine, reached him shortly before his death in August.

It is hard to leave life before one is ready. The closest friend of R.M.S. tells me that of the salutes and guarded farewells which came to him in those final weeks, yours gave him the deepest and most special joy; perhaps, in resolving a cadence so long held in suspension, made it more possible for him to accept.

Looking down now along the perspectives of this golden age of architecture of which you are the central initiating individual source, I find myself wishing to write a retrospective piece.

May I come to Taliesin West to see you?

I think of being in Phoenix in mid-October—if you should be there at that time, and say yes.

Faithfully,
Pauline [*Schindler*]

October 3, 1953
Pauline G. Schindler
Los Angeles, California

Dear Pauline:

Poor Rudolph.
We will be in Phoenix next November 15th. Come there if you can.
Sincerely,

Frank Lloyd Wright, 1932

Johnson Wax Buildings

Taliesin West

Taliesin West, garden room

Pauson House

V. C. Morris shop, interior

David Wright House

Price Tower

Annunciation Greek Orthodox Church

Frank Lloyd Wright at work on Mile High project

III

THREE CRITICS

In a letter dated November 30, 1922 Mr. Wright wrote to H. P. Berlage, State Architect of Holland: "Good criticism is itself creative and needed by my country more than anything else. We have not enough of the critical spirit."

Like all creative artists, Frank Lloyd Wright took a strong interest in any and all critical appraisals of his work. It was an interest that neither fame nor triumphs would ever diminish. Himself a perceptive writer, he appreciated perceptive criticism, but when criticism became petty or biased, or based on prejudice or ignorance, he swiftly lashed out against it to defend his work. He not only believed in his work, he knew better than anyone else how fully it belonged to his nation, to his age, and to the ages to come. For that reason he was quick to challenge criticism that questioned the overriding value of that work.

Since his early work was geographically confined to the Midwest, mainly in and around Chicago, publication was important to him as a way of letting that work be more widely known. The vast media that exists today did not even vaguely exist then, nor could an artist travel from continent to continent in a day's time to make known his living presence. At the turn of the century publication, even more than exhibition, was the primary means of disseminating work at home and abroad. In Mr. Wright's case, first Germany, then Holland and Japan led the way in the production of critical monographs of his work, which included rare and unique architectural drawings and also photographs of executed buildings.

In the United States his work had its first major critical reception in the Architectural Record, in May, 1908. Illustrations of his drawings and buildings were amply represented in that issue, which included his own text entitled, "In the Cause of Architecture." Later, from 1927 to 1929, the editor of the Record, M. A. Mikkelsen, commissioned Frank Lloyd Wright to write a series of articles to appear every other month under the general heading In the Cause of Architecture.

In 1928 the scholar-critic Henry-Russell Hitchcock devoted an issue of the French journal Cahiers d'Arts to Mr. Wright, with good photographs of his completed buildings and an appraisal that recognized his genius and placed him definitively at the forefront of modern architecture during the first quarter of the twentieth century. In 1932 Hitchcock began to qualify what he had previously written. "But there is no question," he summarized, "that Wright is one of the great architects of our time." Thus "the greatest architect" of a decade before had been re-evaluated as "one of." Henry-Russell Hitchcock had by now taken up the banner for the International movement in architecture.

On the other hand the critic Lewis Mumford was unqualified in his praise of the American architecture of Frank Lloyd Wright. In 1929 in his book The Brown Decades he wrote: "At the very time when the archaic note of colonialism was being emphasized by the fashionable architect, Wright was showing his respect for the actual landscape and the actual problems of his day and locality. Wright has embodied in his work two qualities which will never permanently leave it—a sense of place and a rich feeling for materials."

Proclaiming the preeminence of Mr. Wright was Howard Myers, the editor of the Architectural Forum. Supportive of everything Mr. Wright said and did, he might be termed the uncritical critic. Yet in a sense his critical judgments rendered him the most vulnerable of the three, for the success of the Forum depended upon those judgments.

In this section we have confined ourselves to the three critics cited above. Although they represent among them a range of viewpoints, each is eminent, learned and interesting, according to his own standards. Henry-Russell Hitchcock may be said to represent the International angle of vision; Lewis Mumford that of America; Howard Myers that of the informed general public. Their views are rarely the same, nor are Mr. Wright's attitudes toward, and reactions to, them the same. Yet, all three groups of letters follow a similar pattern. Their tone begins with one of friendliness and hope for a continuation of working together "in the Cause of Architecture." At some point in the duration of the correspondence the letters become tempestuous, stormy. They bristle with antagonism and sometimes resentment—yet there is nothing personal in these conflict letters. The issue is always architecture, more specifically the organic architecture which Mr. Wright believed in with his whole being. Then, after the storm, there is reconciliation and the friendship is resumed. Mr. Wright could not stand to bear a grudge; it was contrary to his nature. So many times he would say to his wife, Olgivanna Lloyd Wright, "I would have slept well last night except for some little fellow in there (tapping his chest) that just kept gnawing away at me."

The same condition existed with many—if not most—of his clients, even when those clients, as in the case of Darwin D. Martin and Lloyd Lewis, were very close, personal friends. The letters to these men reveal that at that point where they threatened the integrity of his work, not consciously but unwittingly so, Mr. Wright became defensive, strong, often angry, to try and bring them back to a better understanding of the work at hand. There was no personal strife involved; what Mr. Wright wanted to preserve for his clients, in many cases also his friends, was the integrity of the idea of the building that was being built. Once that was achieved, the friendship was resumed.

HENRY-RUSSELL HITCHCOCK

With the closing of the Bauhaus by Hitler in 1933, there began a migration of architects and artists from Europe to the United States. Mr. Wright welcomed them, and invariably, as in the case of Erich Mendelsohn and Mies van der Rohe, they came to Taliesin to pay their respects to the man whom they knew was the progenitor of modern architecture, regardless of what direction it was to take in their own work.

A number of American critics, Henry-Russell Hitchcock in the forefront among them, were quick to pick up on this European movement, and at a certain point turned all their attention to these architects as the men of vision and new understanding in architecture. Mr. Wright, who had pioneered all of this in the Larkin Building and Unity Temple, was convinced that the Internationalists were missing the facts of the situation as well as the true significance of his work. He went to some lengths, often energetically, to explain both, and the letters to Henry-Russell Hitchcock that follow present these explanations in vivid detail.

(Undated) 1928
Mr. Russell Hitchcock
New York City, N.Y.

My dear Russell Hitchcock:

I haven't made occasion to properly acknowledge your contribution, in French, to the Cause of Architecture as I see it—or rather as from your view-point, it seems, failed to see it.

Since I have no power to have you taken out and shot at sunrise as a traitor to your country, I might as well make the best of it and try to make a friend of you by being one.

Probably Douglas Haskell's post-mortem in Creative Arts, which I have only just read, is the immediate urge to "make up to you" with the matter sent herewith.

If I am not mistaken, knowing neither of you at all—you are both young and passionately interested in Architecture—inclined to be prophetic and very much "intrigued" at the moment with the Surface and Mass Architecture of the French.

You as "critic," I am sure, would like something authentic from me—the victim of so many critics—in this connection.

I would like to help you to set this pretentious "New" in proper line with the "Old," if I could do so, although the matter seems already far-gone.

At least, herewith, you have America's early contribution (so far as it went to Europe) to Modern Architecture.

I am sending nothing but the original impetus so that you may judge of its initial impact abroad for yourself, on its merits. Your quite natural mistake is neglecting to realize that instead of being finished, my own work is only well begun.

The work itself as it has grown out and grown up in the dozen or more buildings on the draughting boards around me as I write would prove to you, I think, how superficial after all is this pretentious fashion-monger, France, in this matter of Architecture which, by nature, is beyond French depth. It is important to "finish" matters before naturally finished.

Sometime, I hope, you may journey to this neck of the woods, spend a day or two with me digging up the matter that so vitally interests us both, by the roots. I should be very glad, indeed, to have you.

Meantime, believe me your friend nevertheless.

The plates are mildewed as they were wet down when my home here burned down.

February 26, 1932
Mr. Russell Hitchcock
The Museum of Modern Art, New York City

My dear Russell Hitchcock: .

First, thanks for the biography. You intended to give the devil his due and, with so many biographies to write, were generous to him.

But my dear R.H. you read so much you must read rapidly, and writing so many facts concerning so many, naturally enough get them mixed sometimes.

May I count some mistakes?

1: Architecture to me is not any exterior but is the *interior* discipline of organic growth. And while rich in liberty is even more severe in limitation than the discipline you endorse but at the same time more fruitful.

2: There is no "romantic" absolute of Man and Nature in my vocabulary or in my practice. And the faults of those studying my work are those of their own Nature not of the nature of the principles to which I subscribe.

3: Is Froebel's kindergarten a toy, then?

4: The Hillside Home school building is not at Richland Center but at Hillside near Spring Green.

5: I had charge of *all* planning and detailing in Adler and Sullivan's office for some four years except direct engineering and field work. Residences were overflow and were outside office-hours. (Your statement would indicate they had a domestic department in my charge and that was my function there, which is wrong.)

6: By the time I broke with Adler and Sullivan I had only *designed* (not built) five houses for the firm and had *built* four on my own overtime with scant superintendence. (I had not *built* 15 houses.) The Winslow house was my first house on my own.

7: There is no lack of light in the Mid Western houses. On the contrary a soft diffusion of light most agreeable to live with. The first owners used to complain of too much light.

8: The decoration of the Coonley House walls is not painted. It is "opus sectilae," a colored tile-mosaic tooled into the plaster wall and partly in relief. As true architectural expression of pattern in materials as any in existence, both authentic and integral.

9: The Larkin Building was consciously the first great protestant that awakened your European Internationalists. They have capitalized the *protest* not in point of style but as a style.

10: Unity Temple is floodlighted from the top as well as from the tempered sides. As light as day. "Gloomy" is a wrong surmise.

11: The Midway Gardens were by the nature of their function a phantasia. If European architects choose to make houses like "fest salles"—why blame the influence? Would you have had the playgardens wear a severe expression?

12: The Barnsdall house ornament is as appropriate as the house itself. If the house is inappropriate then the ornament is so. It looks more like California itself to me than anything I've seen there yet, with all its faults.

13: The block houses are richly ornamented because it is a natural machine age resource to give life to an otherwise characterless surface. A principle is at work. No caprice.

14: The true value of the Jones house, as the vanished wall and the significant freedom that may accompany standardization in the Machine age, you throw entirely away.

15: My work changes with materials and processes naturally. But steel and glass and concrete are not all of modern architecture, it is devoutly to be hoped. Just because they are wholly new it is easiest to be *new* with them. That is all.

16: I am not so sure "the Europeans have come at the same time to realize the advantage of tenuous supports," for nowhere is the principle at work as architecture in anything I have seen as European. Won't you show me?

17: St. Mark's Tower is not based on a scheme of triangles but upon a square contained within a square. One turned opposite to the other. There is no comparison with Bauhaus or any other "haus." If you will study tenuity as at work in this design you will say so and see for once a complete organic expression in structure of an architectural idea.

And may I say my dear R.H. with no lack of appreciation of your critical faculties, which I believe sincere though meticulous, that you do not get inside architecture as an organic expression of the nature and character of materials with infinite possibilities of expansion—but remain a highly intelligent observer of effects with a very definite and aristocratic taste of your own.

The greatest proof I could give Russell Hitchcock of my appreciation of his "biography" is to take it up with him point by point as I have now done.

We see too little of each other—each for his own good? Some day we may remedy that if the "bump" of principle doesn't break us. Perhaps I am going to pray some day that somebody convert me to pragmatism or shoot me.

Sincerely yours,

September 15, 1937
Mr. Russell Hitchcock
Wesleyan University, Middletown, Connecticut

My dear Russell-Hitchcock:

For sometime past when I would run across some pronouncement of yours in current magazines I've wanted to sit down and write you a friendly letter, but I have too little time to devote to a matter of that sort.

Since you choose to write on the topic why do you not devote some years of your life to learning something of architecture? Your knowledge is so superficial, related only to some predilection you have for certain effects which please you which makes them right and certain effects which displease you which makes them wrong.

Now in this connection it is well to ask just who is this Hitchcock? Did he happen or did he grow—what does he know? Is he the usual guesser writing to be noticed—right or wrong—or is he a sincere student of his subject prematurely sharing his personal and inquisitive impressions (in a man of your type they would be "convictions") with all and sundry.

I have been amazed at the continual effrontery of your dicta when I see so plainly the serene negation, and recognize the depths of ignorance beneath it, of all I have myself learned of architecture except certain effects preceding from my own work which you have observed in the works of Le Corbusier, Ludwig Mies, Oud and some others.

Inasmuch as they have taken some pains to inform themselves concerning the nature of this thing I myself call architecture and proceed accordingly, why don't you do the same? We will take you as an apprentice at Taliesin for a year and see if we can't put some fundamental understanding of the great art you only serve to abuse and confuse into the empty hole that it seems to be where super knowledge should be. Were you to become a justified professional critic, which is what your books and articles would seem to indicate you desire to be, something of the sort ought to appeal to your conscience, if not to your taste.

My country is unfortunately cursed by these superficial short cuts to celebrity one of which you have pursued with such persistence and determination. I don't really believe there is much to be done about it—but I make the suggestion for what it may be worth. The suggestion that you inform yourself at the source of the inspiration of those whose work you capitalize is not sarcastic. It is serious. We have met, you and I, and I have recognized a certain dogmatic Presbyterian force of character and personality in you which might serve a good purpose if it went right and do harm if it went wrong.

Our movement in the direction of an organic architecture has suffered a terrible set back from the exploitations of the left wing of which you are a camp follower.

I would like to see you try at least to understand why this is so.

Sincerely yours,

July 12, 1938
Mr. Henry-Russell Hitchcock
Wesleyan University, Middletown, Connecticut

My dear Russell Hitchcock:

Yours is a master hand at heaping coals of fire.

Mrs. Wright and I enjoyed your hospitality. It was perfect. Your establishment taught me more of you than I knew.

Russell, did I by any chance leave the Wesleyan Kudos around there somewhere? We haven't them, anyway.

Kindly remember me to the master of the university and we look forward to a visit from you this fall.

Sincerely yours,

February 18, 1953
Mr. Russell Hitchcock
New York City, N.Y.

Russell:

Where is the brain above those whiskers. Have just read your specious American Bauhaus rationalizations in the book "BUILT IN U.S.A.: POST WAR ARCHITECTURE" just published by the "Haus." There (in the "Haus") is undoubtedly where you belong. I nominate you for Director.

I never felt you were quite comfortable with me because you were never sure of what I was all about. Less than ever do you see now. As Gropius is a scientist, not an architect nor an artist, so you are an historian, not an interpreter nor an artist. As for Mies, he is back there with the organic American negation, therefore 27 years behind the Organic Architecture which was the foundation of his building. You speak of the foundation of his building as passé. Then what about the building?

As Bauhaus propaganda goes (now), the day of the great Architect in America is over, if the Bauhausers can manage. We Americans now, by way of Hitchcock and Johnson, sell ourselves to European standardizations and team work of plan factories when the great Architecture of the individual free should really be our concern, if we are a Democracy. There will be some touting of "the boys in the back room" for a time—the slaves. "Suffer it to be so now."

Great Architecture may succumb for a decade to (German) philosophic degeneracy (collectivism fit for communism). With their kind, Hitchcock and Johnson join again to try to sell Organic American Architecture down stream. But the Bauhaus is definitely now downstream. You may still be here to see Organic Architecture rise even higher because of the "activity" you credit to me. Perhaps confused but none the worse for whatever interim may be. Only Organic Architecture can prevail....

Meantime, go see the "corkscrew museum": Bauhaus epithet of the neophyte Drexler to help me build the new Museum. This word for the opus shows how much the Bauhaus really wants to see that building built.

So, au revoir, Russell...I have loved thee in my fashion. You are back there again where you belong because on that level you can believe. I bid you better luck this time, though your cause is definitely dated as you say you once thought mine to be.

                              Affection, nevertheless,

November 19, 1957
Mr. Russell Hitchcock
New York City, N.Y.

Dear Russell,

Our paths cross again in your cross review of the Testament in the Times. I wish to thank you for the restraint manifested by my old critic who did me as little harm as was consonant with his commitments to others. A critic always has them. I have one dispute only—kindergarten tables at seven, not nine. Since I have always maintained that Russell knows all about everything and (where I am concerned) understands nothing—I mention this.

The "criticism" brings back to me the good old days "in the making" when we were often together and yours was a hand "up," not "out." Couldn't you come out to Taliesin West sometime this winter—bring a friend—why not Philip?—for a friendly wrangle over consequences—and beyond modern architecture at least.

Affection, Russell—
Frank Lloyd Wright

March 8, 1958
Mr. Russell Hitchcock
New York City, N.Y.

Dear Russell:

Thanks for your kind letter. You will remember James McNeil Whistler's "crack"—"I can take care of my enemies, but the Lord deliver me from my friends"? He and I are the only two artists accorded a one-man show at the Paris Beaux Arts, so they told me there. I am sure those in the "eye of the vox populi" get more satisfaction from their enemies, if only the enemy be honest—and I too cherish my enemies if for no other reason than the one the boy gave who said that he didn't mind having the toothache because it felt so good when it stopped.

The architectural profession can't afford to fall out with each other—for fear an honest public may then get its dues?

I am glad to know your absence from the dinner with Philip was really due to illness. I was for some reason anxious about you and was reassured by Philip, who warned me to leave you to him. I suppose it was because after all we have been something to each other not easily discounted as life runs its course.

I've hated internationalism in architecture with as lusty a hate as the enthusiasms with which you embraced it. And I've always felt you were not sure of what organic architecture meant. But the argument is still interesting and worth a man's good time?

So next time I get to New York (Taliesin East is an apartment at the Plaza) let's get together for a good drink and an even better dinner.

Affection,

LEWIS MUMFORD

Lewis Mumford was the first American critic to see into the character of Organic Architecture, to perceive its significance, and to write well about it. In an article for *The New Yorker* in 1939, concerning Fallingwater, the home for Mr. and Mrs. Edgar Kaufmann at Mill Run, Pennsylvania, he wrote: "Whether it was Wright or his client who thought of building a house over a waterfall I do not know, but Wright's imagination played with the opportunity as freely as Michelangelo's played with the decoration of the Sistine Chapel. The perpetual youngness and freshness of his mind were never better shown than in his treatment of this extraordinary problem. The site would have frightened any conventional architect out of his wits. Wright uses the opportunity to demonstrate that when the need arises he can swing a cantilever across space, using the method of construction not as a cliche of modernism but as a rational engineering solution of a real problem.

"One looks at two-dimensional compositions and exhausts them in a view or two, but one must go through Wright's work, finding new compositions, new revelations, new relationships at every step. Even abstractly considered, the planes and the profiles in Fallingwater (as the place is called) are in a state of continuous animation."

Mumford the critic became a close personal friend, and many times Mr. and Mrs. Wright were guests at the Mumford home in Amenia, New York. But when the Second World War began, Mumford took the stand that America should enter the war; Mr. Wright felt that no man dedicated to culture could in any way condone war. The argument over this became a strong one between the two of them, colored even their views on architecture, and eventually the friendship suffered. But the death of Mumford's son in the war brought about a reconciliation, and their friendship was resumed after ten years.

April 30, 1928
Mr. Lewis Mumford
Amenia, N. Y.

My dear Lewis Mumford:

Fiske Kimball has just sent me a copy of his new book. A well written brief for the "Classic," bracketing McKim, Meade and White's thought in Architecture with Louis Sullivan's—God save the mark! And this is "history."

It would be hard to beat that for grave robbing, I say. I write this because of a note from the Century Company, asking for views of "Taliesin" to illustrate my article on "American Architecture" in which you make "a kindly reference to me." (See copy of enclosed letter to Fiske Kimball.)

I am heartily sick of the historical falsifying of the real course of ideas in the Architecture of our Country, unconsciously done as most of it is. A true concept of "modernism" in origin or effect is so far almost wholly lacking. Why don't you record it? No man has yet, stood up to this task, learning anything further West of Manhattan, the commercialized monstrosity, than Buffalo, New York.

Why not you come afield and see for yourself the healthy undergrowth coming through this rank obscuring growth of pseudo-classic weeds. A healthy undergrowth rising from seed planted in the prairie soil thirty years ago?

You will write what you please, but until you have "come" afield, led by myself, you will not write with more than the outside instinct which is dangerous in a historian, unless based upon the fundamental acts contributing to the subject he views and records. Pardon the seeming attempt to "preach." It is perhaps uncalled for and an egotistic assumption on my part, but I am just smarting from Fiske Kimball's well-meant "obituary."

Faithfully yours,

January 7, 1929

Dear Lewis Mumford:

You will be glad to know I am no longer walking the New York streets, hat in hand. Taliesin is regained. We are established here, again at work—interesting work—not to brag about it, but to reassure you; am working on the Desert-Resort Hotel in the Simon-pure Arizona desert. Half million dollar commission, for Dr. Chandler at Chandler, Arizona near Phoenix—cactus among the cacti, nearby where I established the textile-block construction in the "million dollar" Arizona Biltmore, now nearing completion; in a new house in spirit and letter for my editor cousin at Tulsa, Oklahoma; a twenty-three story copper and glass apartment-tower for your barbaric New York City—St. Mark's Tower in-the-Bouwerie—"the architect triumphant over the Machine," let us hope; a school house for the Rosenwald Foundation, you know, the Negroes in the South. I have tried to make this one theirs. The Yankee things they have been getting seem to me rather hard on them. This is another modest excursion into the nature and feeling of an alien race such as was the Tokyo hotel on a grand scale.

Have also signed a life contract with Leerdam Glass-fabriek to make glass designs for all sorts of things on a royalty basis. Trying my hands at the arts and crafts, you see.

Read the prospectus of the school herewith and write me a "brief." The University is already interested. Your supporting word would help. Enough here you see, to show the Frenchmen some of the things they inadvertently overlooked.

The enclosed to Douglas Haskell will tell you all of that story. I shall have to look to you for rescue in the end. I knew I would.

It seems the coroner's jury is sitting and both Hitchcock and Haskell are there in behalf of "Surface and Mass." The jury so far seems rather negligent of the more vital factors involved in an architecture for America. But that's the way the wind is blowing just now.

I am sending on the last article touching this subject written for the [Architectural] Record because I can see the fight coming on and I might as well speak my mind on that subject. As yet, it seems to have had no mind applied to it directly.

As for myself, I was tired of working with lame methods. My hands were sore with makeshift tools. No wonder I threw down the walls of circumstance now and then. At least my countrymen already have from me valid evidence of power. And how silly and ungrateful to brand as weakness the radiation of character from my work. Just in proportion to his force, the artist will find his work outlet for his proper character, says Emerson. But no mannerist could have made my varied group of buildings? I cannot hope, nor should I want to emancipate myself from, my age and my country. And this quality in my work will have a higher charm, a greater value than any individual quality could have.

The New in art is always formed out of the Old.

Art does exhilarate and its aim is truly no less than the creation of man as a perfect follower of nature. What an excursion! As yet, however, I had never been really frivolous.

Now as a student of the mystery of form, I have found an outlet for all my energy.

No need to ask what is the mode in Paris.

Nothing confounds the critic, it seems, like common sense or straightforward dealing of any kind. He is taken in by surface indications of it and fails to see it as a reality beneath an exuberance.

I hope Melville is born and parturition none too devastating.

That happy look of youth you wore when last I saw you should never be impaired.

Here's a snapshot made a few days ago—it happens to be lying on my drawing board. I send it to show you how I've wasted away since we last met—that look of "battered up but still in the ring."

Tell me how all goes with you. Yesterday someone told me that truly-old I.K. Pond took exception in print to your "Sticks and Stones" because you weren't a "practicing architect." What "practicing architects" know anything at all of Architecture anyway, even if they could write about it? Certainly not he.

He's a dried herring, hanging beneath the eaves of Architecture.

Don't bother, but when the spirit moves, drop me a line. I believe in your genius and see great things ahead of you. Wish I could hurry them up—but you are young. Stay so by creative work. It is the only sure way.

That book of which you spoke is now imminent. We are working on one to be published by the Record, another by any one of several New York publishers.

I could use that promised article of yours in this connection as you suggested and be grateful.

It has occurred to me that you might be interested to have the plates from the monograph (I have a great many loose plates which made their appearance in Germany in 1910. Of course many of them were designed some years before). In these I think you may see "Surface and Mass" prophetic. Many German architects, Mendelsohn among them, have told me that these things burst on their vision with an uplift in their own present direction that was tremendous.

I enclose again a clipping from Los Angeles Times—the paper that is to the west coast what the New York Times is to the east coast—that takes the right attitude toward this French propaganda of Lee Simonson et al.

December 17, 1930

My dear Lewis Mumford:

I've been wondering if you've forgotten the Mendelsohn, or only are just busy as the happy consequence of a well-deserved success.

Since seeing you I've read 'The Golden Day' and Melville, winding up with 'Moby Dick.' I had a good time and feel I know you quite well now. Your Melville is quite worthy Moby Dick himself. A very fine study—years—in that work.

I wish I, myself, could write. As it is, I am to be "lecturer." Princeton asks me to come and deliver the course this coming May, and ask to publish. Inasmuch as I shall receive money for the lectures I close my "amateurship." Yes, now I am a lecturer "Singularly doomed to what we execrate and writhe to shun." I've saved the day however, by making the seventh an Exhibition of my recent work.

We are designing and setting it up here with an idea of letting it leave Princeton en tour of the U.S.A. We are giving it careful attention, making models as well as drawings using fresh old material, as well. You know Lewis I am sorry I called poor Hitchcock a fool and am writing to take back a swipe at his latest book I wrote for the Record.

Why should I try to hurt him? He is at least sincere. What if he doesn't know? He may learn. Anyhow, I can't strike the blow. It is not to my taste.

I hope you are as well as you looked the last time I saw you, and mean to come with your wife and child to see us and ours—some day this spring?

(Undated) 1930

My dear Lewis:

I looked all over the place for you without success just before we sat down to dinner and got no chance to talk with you the night of the

"League" to thank you for your excellent talk at the table. The others were meant to be "high wide and handsome" and somewhat were, but you said the things to be said, as you usually do.

I can think of little else very well worth remembering except the spectacle of our hardboiled New Yorkers coming across for our little homemade show.

I am again indebted to you for your vision and courage; before long I should begin to "come back to you." At Princeton I was asked on several different occasions—what do you think of Lewis Mumford (showing you were on their minds out there). My answer was, "The most valuable critic our country has—a mind of Emersonian quality—with true creative power." Said my hostess one evening, "But don't you think the young man too "cocksure"? "Not of anything he doesn't actually grasp," I said...

The New York boys backed up their enthusiasm by refusing to let me pay for my expenses to and from New York or for entertainment while there or for any costs in connection with the show at all. Moreover, they say to me there is a genuine desire on their part to take me "in" on the Chicago fair in some way where I can be really useful. What that way is I don't know yet. Corbett, Walker, Hood, and Kahn give me this much advance notice. But please understand my dear Lewis, I am really uncomfortable with this "recognition." Am I really losing my power and so they are no longer afraid of me? I shall have to go carefully from now on—not recklessly as before. Doing a "Lindberg" in architecture is more fun in itself than any of its consequences can ever be.

Have heard nothing from Scribner's about the "book"—but soon I suppose.

In a year from now my dear man! Meantime—"all I can."

April 27, 1935

Dear Lewis:

I've just read "Wright's City" in the New Yorker and find you trying rather hard to be nice to me. At least so it seemed to me as I read. I am sorry we couldn't have gone into Broadacres a little more thoroughly because the main value of the whole thing save architecturally is quite missed in your criticism.

I don't know what you can mean by preferring the German tenement and slum solution as preferable to the Broadacre's minimum house and maximum of space.

There can be no possible comparison between the two as to privacy, light and air, living accommodations—or what have you—at $600.00.

Add to that, that the tenement unit in the rank and file in Broadacres becomes a complete individual little free holding no less sightly and dignified in quality as an individual home than those near it having more of material resources.

And, I must confess, you puzzle me Lewis. When you have time (I suppose you have little enough) please explain. Will you? You might teach me something I ought to know.

Affectionately,

April 29, 1941

Dear Lewis:

We will be glad to see you this summer whenever the spirit moves you to stop with us.

It is a real pain to me to find ourselves in disagreement. I know little of politics. What opinions I hold are based only upon principles I apprehend. So I am sure we have no quarrel outside what expedients to employ.

Faithfully as always,

June 3, 1941

A REPLY TO AN ATTACK FROM LEWIS MUMFORD. A LETTER WHICH HE IMMEDIATELY POSTED TO THE EDITOR OF "THE LEADER," A PRO-WAR PAPER.

My dear Lewis:

When, because of a difference of feeling and judgement, you can shamelessly insult one who has trusted your sincerity, admired your ability, and praised you as a manly man, well, Lewis, I can understand your anguish and desire for revenge—but I say such reactions as yours are certainly not trustworthy when and wherever the welfare of our nation is at stake—I believe it to be, and you say you believe it to be, in danger.

Be ashamed, Lewis, some day—but take your time. I am human grass roots in the service of the culture of a beloved country. I can give you time.

For the same reason that I despise eclecticism and reaction I despise your attitude toward war and Empire. There is no good Empire; there never was a just war. I despise your attitude now as I despised the setting sun all Europe mistook for dawn. It was called the "Renaissance."

If going to war is now your way, you have never really settled anything for yourself nor ever will settle anything for anyone else. Yours is the mind that would throw the dead cat back and forth across the backyard fence.

And I don't mean what you mean when I say "I love English." I love my England. You love yours. I hate master-empire or slave-empire. So my England is not your England and I am thankful.

You prate of culture, Lewis. Organic character is the basis of true greatness in that or in any individual concern or in any nation. War is the negation of this potentiality now as ever and forever. You knew that and yet sometime ago you wrote to me that you "had been busy getting the United States ready to fight and having accomplished that to your satisfaction you were ready to go back and write another book."

Christ, Lewis, is it possible that you are unable to see your own hypocrisy? Why do you try to hide behind what you call mine?

No honest believer in truth or beauty in his right mind could do what you say you have done. Time will discover you a deserter. A traitor on a battle-field that did you honor only to discover in you a vengeful, conceited writer, another writer out of ideas. The Chinese say it well: "He who runs out of ideas first strikes the first blow."

You standing for the time-cursed expedient with the frightened crowds! What a disappointment! And yet I could take it all from you because you are young and still be your friend if I believed you sincere in your anguish and desire for revenge. But you are not.

You prate of "downtrodden democracies" and of "defending slaves," only to justify your own impotence and rage. Why not honestly examine your own heart? What you would see there is what you accuse me of...hypocrisy.

Listen my young friend! I liked to call up and talk to you occasionally when I got to the great city but I see now that you, too, are yellow with this strange but ancient sickness of the soul: the malady that has thrown down civilization after civilization by meeting force with force. Is meeting force with force the only way you see? Then I am sorry for you—you amateur essayist on culture. It is not the only way I see. I—a builder—see that there is still a chance for democracy on this continent just because the leaders of our culture are not all like Lewis Mumford, as he snarls and shows his teeth now.

Goodbye, Lewis, I shall read your "brief" in The New Yorker with shame. I shall read it knowing your real opinion is worthless whatever you may write.

July 10, 1951

Dear Lewis:

Your letter has weeded our garden and the flowers are showing as fresh and beautiful as after a spring rain. The weeds are gone. By the roots.

I've missed you Lewis. Yours is an Emersonian mind but on your own terms. What a man he was and how we need such—now. I've read your little book and what a man you are. I shall never cease to be aware of the fact that I owe to you primal appreciation and support when it took real courage for you to render it. *That* I count as one of the real honors that have "fallen into my lap." As for the others, well—only those similar (they are rare) have any effect. Italy is such and took us to the Italian heart. We have just returned. Zevi spoke warmly of you and regretted the break between us. I assured him there was one no longer.

Now how soon can you—will you—bring your wife and daughter for a week with us here at Taliesin Mid-west?

We have a pleasant guest-house in the hill-garden ready for you. Why not motor out (or fly out) and do say when?

I want to see you and we want you to see how we work here. In addition to mine you would find a great welcome here—all around. When will you shake off the urban shackles and come to our country-home for a week?

Send me the little memorial to the lost son.

As ever,

January, 1952

My dear Llewis:

Refusing my earnest invitation to come help Taliesin fills me with a vague fear—a fear that I shall, never again, meet the Llewis I loved—he who lived and wrote out of love and understanding, let fall what might—my valiant, vibrant, independently honest Llewis—the Mumford.

I now see you have been more badly hurt than I supposed and that therefore I may meet a broadened but wisened professionalized writer with the if's but's and also's of his craft, temporizing for fame, himself a slave of livelihood.

Because my Llewis, no matter what, would not plead "engagement" when asked with love to come to this capitol of the modern world of Architecture to share *experience* with love and understanding of this work he was bound to cherish. (Yes, I refer to this little America within America we call Taliesin)—a work he has never seen, where he would naturally feel and be at home with what he loved as his own.

And Llewis—how richly well Taliesin could afford to transport you and your Sophie to this architecture of the Valley of the Sun—plant you both in a little cottage here (your own for a fortnight) asking only that you talk to the boys at Sunday morning breakfast and let them talk to you and answer their queries Sunday evening.

If you drive yourself you would have an M.G. to wander about wild Arizona. Of if you don't drive—a Chrysler and driver to take you. Between times as the spirit moved we could talk or not talk as we used to do. And then we would send you back by way of Frisco, if you wanted to go that way, to experience the Morris shop.

You have never seen the work of these later years.

Well here you see the arrogance you find in me because I suppose you could have no "engagement" that could matter enough to hold you away from that experience in the circumstances. You see, Llewis, being so sure of my ground and my star so early in life, I was soon forced to choose between honest arrogance and a hypocritical humility.

Well, the world knows I chose honest arrogance. Nor am I sorry. Nor is my Cause. You didn't use to mind? You do mind now, because, well, you have so said.

And so, I fear, that he—the Llewis of my youth—is no more. Suddenly I am afraid I shall find in his place the professionalized successful Critic with unbreakable engagements—an E. M. Forster critic (see his last book "Two Cheers for Democracy" and read his piece on the "Raison d'etre of Criticism," if you have not already read it). You will see there what I mean.

No, you have never really *experienced* the creative work into which the work of those early years developed. I don't think a man like you needs drink a tub of dye to know what color it is—but—because there was love and understanding between us that is why the rupture was so violent. Whatever the Llewis may now be that I am to meet in New York about the first of February, though the same old depth may no longer apply, yet there may be something precious to preserve?

At any rate, like a man hungry for the honesty of the romantic understanding that is courageous love, I shall be grateful and pleasant as I know you will be for whatever may be left.

Llewis, "engagements" in such circumstances as I propose are a cruel bond. Are we too old to break them to play hookey once more?

Arrogant as ever—you see?—with the same old affection and a new nostalgia.

By the way, do you reprove me for the ancestral double I by never using it yourself?

December 18, 1953

Dear Lewis:

Olgivanna has just read your New Yorker accolade to me. Lewis, I now understand, for the first time, why you have never been to Taliesin, East or West, and that the old sore still rankles in your mind. The fatal difference between us seems to lie in everyone for the commonplace instead of the commonplace for everyone as something to rise above by his innate strength of inspiration.

Communism versus Democracy; quality above quantity? But no doubt now, you have blessed everyone but your victim which is what the critic usually considers his privilege, if not his sacred duty. The International Style wins. It seems to have found a friend in you. But I am really astonished to see you put the cart before the horse—giving the works of the Europeans precedence when it really belongs to us because of my work appearing there in 1910 (eleven years previous), which does not seem to interest you, for some reason.

As for humanist-qualities, consider Broadacre City again for just that. And—you might take a look at the Taliesin Fellowship itself for a valid humanitarian-impulse in my work, on my part, if so inclined.

As a matter of fact the humanities are dead against your judgements all down the line of your criticism. This will someday become even more evident, I believe.

Yes, the old quarrel comes uppermost again! How sad. Does the exercise of the critical-faculty require a bias of some kind? I never realized how little—in detail—you really "took-in" of my real significance as an architect, to myself, to my time or to you and yours—in my work.

Nevertheless, my best to Sophie, and Allison and yourself.

Affection as always more from the
Democrat to the Socialist...

Lewis! What really hurts is to know that you—to whom I have looked with hope and love—should understand my work so much in reverse.

May 22, 1958

Dear Lewis:

Olgivanna and I have often discussed the fact that the Mumfords have never honoured either of the Taliesins with a sojourn—of any kind. Why is this true? I have no answer. In truth, there is none explicable—or ethical—so it must be moral? Now that daughter is married and if Sophie were reconciled, you two may be comparatively free to roam—why do we not plan a few days going over auld lang syne and see what we at Taliesin have ploughed into this valley—a choice example of what Southern Wisconsin would be like were no poles and wires along the valley-roads, the right kind of buildings for the right kind of people in the right places...and how liberally all this adds up to humanity in possession of its birthright.

You would be completely by yourselves to carry on whatever work you desired, for as long or short a time as the spirit claimed.

We would take care of any expense incurred because of a talk or two with the friendly youth inhabitating part of Taliesin—this as you might decide would be merely incidental or not at all.

We have growing pains and are badly oversized. Your views on the young college of Architecture my will is establishing would be especially welcome to me at this time.

My best to you both in the way of
affection and appreciation,

June 4, 1958

Dear Llewis:

Don't be a dear old mule—I am beginning to feel that you are afraid of me: afraid you might lose some of the cherished beliefs regarding attitudes, predilections, affections and predetermined philosophy of mankind: don't want to expose yourself to contamination—or argument?

But I know there must be some cause of absence—some other reasons less egotistic and futile. I understand a man's absorption in his work to the exclusion of any honor he might bestow upon an old friend by his presence. But this absenteeism I fear has other causes into which I will do well not to "dig." Even if I could, how can I?

Salute! dear Llewis: yours shall remain a cherished secret—incognito in so far as our fellowship goes.

Don't grieve about Allison because she is so lucky to have "found-out" soon enough. There are innumerable discretions as well as indiscretions ahead for your Allison as for our Iovanna.

My level best to your handsome, intelligent wife, Sophie, and as for you, "lieber-Llewis"—look out for the ingrowing of a special talent amounting to genius.

Affection,

Hokusai was ninety-seven and prayed for three years more—if granted, "every dot and every line would be alive." Hiroshige, seventy and the same. All the big old philsophers had white beards hanging below the level of the navel and (I have duly "rapped on wood"—the cross—three times). Here are a few statistics in the region of the vegetable and thrown in: Bernard Shaw—a hundred but for a fall from an apple tree. Etc., etc. Youth is a quality; "young" is a circumstance.

In the Archives at Taliesin there are some handwritten notes by Mr. Wright concerning a dinner given in honor of Lewis Mumford by the American Union of Decorative Artists and Craftsmen of New York. Mr. Wright had written: "He is young in years and he is young in spirit. He is strong and brave. Anyone might say of Lewis as Napoleon said of Goethe: 'Here is a man.' It has been said that Lewis discovered me. If he did I am proud of his company. During the next ten years we will all know whether our culture is the twilight of dawn or the twilight of evening. If Lewis Mumford's work continues as it has begun, it will be sunrise and not sunset. Audac! His health! And may he return with more riches of the same kind. To him a good voyage and safe return to us all."

HOWARD MYERS

The Architectural Record had long been Mr. Wright's favorite journal in the profession of architecture, but in 1936 Howard Myers, editor of the Forum, approached Mr. Wright for the rights to an exclusive publication of the Johnson Wax Administration Building. It marked the beginning of a matchless ten year friendship. "Co-workers in the vineyard of the Lord" was the way Mr. Wright liked to describe his association with Howard Myers. The two special Frank Lloyd Wright issues of the Forum, January 1938 and January 1948, were the result of Myers' efforts, work, and constant campaigning. His magazine championed Mr. Wright's work continuously, the Wrights and Myers visited back and forth whenever possible, and the deep bond that arose between the two men strengthened with the passing of time.

November 27, 1936
Frank Lloyd Wright, Architect
Taliesin, Spring Green, Wisconsin

My dear Mr. Wright:

Tom Maloney has been kind enough to transmit your wire in response to our request for publishing rights on your new building for the Johnson Company, of Racine.

To conform to the stern realities of publishing, may I indicate what we should like to have and you can then let me know whether such an arrangement meets with your approval.

It has long been the policy of THE FORUM to publish material exclusively whenever possible and, on those rare occasions when that is not possible, to publish it prior to its appearance in any other architectural or building magazine. We shall, therefore, require either exclusive or prior use of

1. your own story interpreting the building
2. plans and working drawings showing details of the most interesting features
3. exterior and interior photographs

in return for which THE FORUM agrees to

1. reimburse you for the above in the amount of $500

2.   publish the material in a manner consistent with its importance and with THE FORUM'S handling of feature presentations, which would mean a minimum of sixteen full pages—and very possibly more.

I hope that this arrangement will be satisfactory to you and assure you we look forward with high anticipation to publishing your latest work.

Sincerely,
Howard Myers

December 7, 1936
Mr. Howard Myers, Editor
The Architectural Forum, New York City, N.Y.

My dear Mr. Myers:

I guess I will have to abdicate (I still feel obliged to my old friend Dr. Mikkelsen of the Record who when I was in deeper distress than at present gave me an all time "high" for a series of articles for the Record ("The Nature of Materials") at $500.00 an article in favour of the new FORUM whose acquaintance I have yet to make.

My clients have intimated that they prefer THE FORUM.

So I accept for myself (and for them) your offer as outlined in your letter of November 27th.

I should like to ask, however, that the check for $500.00 be sent on so we can use as much of the sum as is necessary in preparing our end of the article—there are other reasons none of which reflect upon anyone but ourselves—and that the layout and all text concerning it be submitted to me for approval before being published.

As a matter of fact your "all time high" is (I believe) not so high for an article of the importance where our architecture is concerned, which I will be constrained to write. The article will bring forward solutions of many problems vexing modern architects and clear up many ambiguities in many directions. But architecture is not paid as literature is paid. Perhaps it shouldn't be as things are.

Sincerely yours,
Frank Lloyd Wright

December 9, 1936

My dear Mr. Wright:

Your letter of December 7 puts everything in order regarding publication of the Johnson building in THE FORUM and I am pleased to enclose our check for $500 in full payment for this material.

We shall, of course, wish to have your suggestions on the complete presentation before it is published; perhaps you could make a layout for our guidance.

It would help us if you could let me know when the material is likely to be ready so that we can schedule it for the proper month. As I think you know, Tom Maloney hopes to see you over the holidays and he can discuss the matter of photographs with you at that time.

May I say again that we count it a great privilege that you and your client have selected THE FORUM.

Sincerely,
Howard Myers

July 28, 1937

My dear Mr. Wright:

On my return from a short trip, I was delighted to learn through George Nelson that you are in fine health and spirit.

All of us are excited over the proposed Frank Lloyd Wright issue of THE FORUM. We hear much these days that there is no leadership in American architecture; such an issue would definitely refute that view. I hope, therefore, that Nelson has correctly reported your interest in undertaking such an issue and that you will let me know how we might proceed.

My thought would be to plan in terms of approximately seventy pages, starting with your introductory text, which might deal with the current architectural scene—or for that matter, any approach which appeals to you—and then follow with very complete presentations of four or five projects including, I assume, the Johnson Building, the Kaufmann House, and if possible a small inexpensive house, and such others as you may choose.

If this program finds your approval, for what month in 1938 do you suppose we could schedule the issue? And by all means, let me know in what way, if any, THE FORUM'S staff could be of assistance.

Sincerely,
Howard Myers

July 31, 1937

My dear Howard Myers:

Your nice letter makes us want to go on with the special FORUM at once. We will take all the help you will give us. Suggest you run up yourself for a few days while we make the initial line up.

You are right. It is time something was said and done. We'll do it at the earliest moment possible to THE FORUM.

Say the January 1938 number?

Let us know if and when we may expect a visit from you?

Sincerely yours,
Frank Lloyd Wright

October 4, 1937

My dear Frank Lloyd Wright:

Back to my desk and the city, which looks more drab than usual after the visit to Taliesin. There is no way I can tell you in suitably restrained language how thoroughly I enjoyed those hours with you.

I have written Hedrich asking that he get in touch with you immediately regarding photographing Taliesin, the Johnson Building, the Johnson House, the small new house in Madison, the original house in Madison, and—if you like—the other one we looked at. Also I have asked him to arrange with you to photograph the Kaufmann House and, finally, to get prices on air views of Taliesin and the work in Madison, which I am afraid will be over our heads.

You must tell me what is to be done about photographs of the house in Texas, the Dean Malcolm Willey house, the Jacobs house, and the house in Palo Alto.

We will assume that January is to be the month, which means that all material should reach us by December 1, including photographs, plans, special drawings, and text. The maximum number of pages available is seventy-two. Under separate cover I am sending some layout sheets which show page and column dimensions. In no case should the type page exceed 10 1/4 inches in height or 7 1/2 inches in width.

The special cover design which you spoke of can probably be included in THE FORUM and then used later for the book if we can manage to publish a book, which seems a reasonable expectation.

We should shortly announce your issue and it would help me if you could send along a simple outline of contents indicating the order in which the material will appear.

I realize that some of the work will have to appear as drawings but I think you will agree with me that insofar as possible photographs should be used.

Finally, if your plans bring you to New York before you start for Arizona, please let me know in advance so that we can have at least a few minutes together to clear up any questions.

And why shouldn't there be an annual Frank Lloyd Wright issue of THE ARCHITECTURAL FORUM?

Sincerely,
Howard Myers

January 10, 1938

To the Young Man in Architecture—a Challenge:

I have taken over the writing and editing of the January ARCHITEC-TURAL FORUM.

I turned editor partly because Howard Myers came to Taliesin and asked me to—partly because I felt the time had come to restate a few fundamentals which are strangely missing from the contemporary scene.

The days and nights and the long hours I have put into the making of this issue are important only to me. But important to you are the months and years that went into the making of these buildings whose plans and photographs this issue brings you for the first time with critical text.

This ARCHITECTURAL FORUM is the first and only record in print of what we have come to call the modern movement, from its inception to its present interpretation. Some of the buildings shown as examples were built more than forty years ago. Some were recently completed. They were produced under a wide variety of circumstances—both social and economic, and for clients from West to East.

Together they show the basic principles which give vitality and integrity to such architecture as we have. Here in some 100-odd pages of plates, text and plans, you will see architecture as indigenous to America as the earth from which it springs, just as here you will see the futility and dishonesty of trying to transplant to America an architectural veneer which finds its roots in God knows where or what.

It is a sense of the whole that is lacking in the "modern" buildings I have seen, and in this issue we are concerned with that sense of the whole which alone is radical. There is more beauty in a fine ground plan itself than in almost any of its consequences. So plot plans and structural plans have been given due place in this issue as of first importance.

Many of the houses demonstrate the folly of imagining that a true and beautiful house must employ synthetics or steel to be "modern" or go to the factory to be economical. Glass? Yes, the modern house must use glass liberally. Otherwise it may be a simple wood house under a sheet of copper.

I would rather solve the small house problem than build anything else I can think of (except the modern theatre). But where is a better small house to come from while Government housing itself is only perpetuating the old stupidities? I do not believe it will come from current education, from big business or by way of smart advertising experts. It must come from common sense—a pattern for more simple and at the same time more gracious living.

To give the little Jacobs family a sensible house with benefit of the industrial advantages of our era, we must do more than plant for them another little imitation of a mansion.

And so in the January FORUM I have shown a $5500 house—a house with a new sense of space and light and freedom. And this house has no visible roof; no plague-spot of an old-fashioned basement (a steam-warmed concrete mat four inches thick laid directly on the ground over gravel filling is better); no radiators or light fixtures, no painting, no interior trim, no plastering, no gutters, no down-spout, no garage (a carport will do as cars are made today).

In the January FORUM I have also shown a plan for a skyscraper with each floor proceeding outward as a cantilever slab from a concrete core to an enclosing shell of glass and copper—the only urban skyscraper fit for human habitation.

I have shown an office building designed to be as inspiring a place to work in as any cathedral ever was in which to worship—a building which becomes, by way of long glass tubing, crystal, where crystal (either translucent or transparent) is most appropriate.

I have shown my own Taliesin, a house of the North. I have shown a house designed for living down in a glen over a mountain stream. I have shown a house for the rolling prairie, and a home for Texas (Texas needs a Texas house). I have shown a house for California, a house for the desert.

My purpose and hope in presenting this material in the ARCHITEC-TURAL FORUM is to promote discussion and rekindle enthusiasm for an honest American architecture. After months of work on this January issue I am more convinced than ever that this work should prove of value, particularly to the younger architects, who are America's last line of defense.

Here is a challenge; may I see it answered in three dimensions across the country.

Faithfully,
Frank Lloyd Wright

January 11, 1938

Dear Frank,

Last night I sent you two copies of the issue by air mail. By now they should have reached you. I was in some doubt about where to send them because a letter yesterday morning from Professor Hanna indicated that you were in California.

Although the issue has just gone out, I have had two telephone calls and one telegram this morning—needless to say, paeans of praise. My one hope is that it pleases you as much as I am sure it will thousands of others.

I haven't seen the TIME story yet but I have seen a proof of the cover and it is a knockout. There is also to be a January FORUM advertisement on the inside cover of LIFE this week.

Shortly before Christmas we got together a little box which we expressed to Taliesin. This, I presume, did not reach you before you left so I trust you will find its contents unblemished upon your return.

As you may know, we have been visited by Edgar Tafel and Charles Samson. I hope that all of your boys and girls will understand that a warm welcome is always here for them.

Our first snow dropped in on us this morning and I was happy to make a handsome appearance in the muffler, which graciously showed at least no outward resentment at being shifted from such important shoulders—I fully expected it to shrivel at the sight of its proud new owner.

Sincerely, with warm regards to all—
Howard

January 31, 1938

Dear Howard:

Inasmuch as we unexpectedly published the Kaufmann office I forgot to mention the master-craftsman who executed the work.

Herewith Mr. Sandoval: would you put him into your next issue somewhere among errata-Dessert, for instance, instead of Desert in the letter wherein you played Frank Lloyd Wright while I was playing Howard Myers; also *you* made Mr. Thoreau say contrast when *he* said contract—etc.

Concerning Sandoval please say for me: owing to unexpected publication of Kaufmann Senior's business office while still uncompleted, I omitted to mention the name of the master-craftsman who executed that work—Manuel Sandoval, Nicaragua, one of the earliest members of the Taliesin Fellowship.

Sincerely,
Frank

February 7, 1938
Frank Lloyd Wright, Architect
Taliesin in the Desert

Dear Frank,

I have always understood that great men cannot spell for a damn so I was not at all surprised when I discovered that you had written "dessert" instead of "desert." What form of vengeance Mr. Thoreau will take on both of us, I leave to your more active imagination.

Mr. Sandoval appears to be both aggressive and brawny so we shall give him his just due in the next issue, March.

Cordially,
Howard

JULY 7, 1938
HOWARD MYERS—

ARCHITECT'S LICENSE DEMANDED FOR HOUSE IN GREAT NECK. HOW DO I GO ABOUT GETTING ONE? AM LICENSED IN ILLINOIS AND WISCONSIN—ISN'T THAT ENOUGH? WOULD YOU HAVE ONE OF YOUR BOYS INVESTIGATE—AND THANK YOU SO MUCH.

FRANK

JULY 8, 1938
FRANK LLOYD WRIGHT
TALIESIN

NEW YORK REQUIRES WRITTEN APPLICATION FOLLOWED BY ORAL EXAMINATION, WHICH IN YOUR CASE WOULD SIMPLY BE A FORMALI- TY BUT NECESSARY UNDER THE LAW. AND THE NEW YORK BOARD DOES NOT MEET UNTIL SEPTEMBER. APPLICATION BLANK BEING FOR- WARDED IN CASE YOU ELECT TO DO THIS. ALSO UNDERSTAND THAT ANY ARCHITECT REGISTERED IN NEW YORK WHO SIGNED YOUR PLANS WOULD PROBABLY HAVE HIS LICENSE REVOKED. BEST SUGGES- TION IS YOU COMMUNICATE WITH WISCONSIN STATE BOARD AND APPLY FOR A NATIONAL COUNCIL RATING WHICH WOULD AUTOMATICALLY MAKE YOU ELIGIBLE IN MOST STATES INCLUDING NEW YORK. THIS MIGHT BE FASTER AS NATIONAL COUNCIL OFFICES ARE IN CHICAGO. ADVISE IF ANYTHING FURTHER I CAN DO.

HOWARD

September 9, 1939

Dear Howard:

This is about as tardy as my apologies ought to be.

My appointment at 4 P.M. with ourselves at your office didn't come off because I was far away, asleep.

I trust this will make everything all right—inasmuch as you had to be there anyway.

Faithfully,
Frank

September 30, 1939

Dear Frank:

This acknowledgement of your September ninth note does not prove that I can outdo you in tardiness, but was occasioned by a long (almost two weeks) trip to the Pacific Coast. I do not resent the fact that you preferred sleeping to an engagement with me, but I resent thoroughly your preferring to sleep elsewhere rather than in my office, in view of the fact that I have provided a most comfortable divan for your exclusive use.

The best thing I saw in Los Angeles was your son Lloyd. He isn't quite so handsome as his pater, but much more so than a lot of those lovely glamour boys who live right around the corner from his attractive home. He showed me a little model of his desert house, which is indigenous as hell and will doubtless prove much more comfortable as a place of residence.

With Harwell Harris I visited the Barnsdall house, which is now serving as a museum, and also another of your houses on a hillside that is still occupied by the original tenant whose name escapes me. In any event he hasn't escaped you as he told me that, after living in the house for some 15 years, he is more convinced than ever that you are the best damned architect in the world. That struck me as rank understatement. Harwell Harris, by the way, is a coming young fellow. His houses, all of them small and inexpensive, fit their sites and have none of that nudity which has never impressed me as the most gracious manner in which to receive one's guests.

I drove down with some other people from San Francisco to Palo Alto and saw the Hanna house from the outside only. My friends told me that they had been so rebuffed by the Hannas on several previous occasions when they tried to get in that there was no point to making the attempt. However, sometime we can go out there together, and you can sneak me in in your pocket.

Los Angeles impressed me as unspeakably dull; San Francisco I found very exciting. Also, I like the Northern California people so much better. They seem to know why they are there and what they are doing. In addition, San Francisco can boast a really inventive architect in the person of Timothy Pflueger. Until about a year ago, Timothy had never been abroad so that he has had to figure things out all by himself. He has gobs of personal vitality and integrity, and it shows in his work. You have to have it to get the San Francisco Stock Exchange to put a Rivera mural at the head of its grand staircase, and it's still there.

So here I am back home. In case of war....as Roger Allen remarked the other day, "Just to think that all this mess was started by a guy who wasn't even smart enough to be an architect." Or as a nice British lady said to my cousin before she sailed from London a couple of weeks ago, "I do wish that man Hitler would marry and settle down."

Come on down and see us, and we'll have some fun while there's still some around.

Cordially,
Howard

—and when do we *start* on the next issue?

January 12, 1940

My dear Howard:

First—I much appreciate your gift (the Sandburg). Olgivanna and the Fellowship said the chocolates in tiers were the best they ever ate. It's high time some recognition of all these kind thoughts for us besides language reached you and Mrs. Myers. Next Christmas is our turn.

Your note mentioning the 500 just read with understanding. I suspected it Howard but I wasn't sure until you said it. I've noted your reactions and noticed their effects while apparently ignoring them.

In this portfolio of 27 modest cost houses for another Forum I think we are heading into something neither of us can afford. It might break us both. So let's drop it as it is probably all out of scale.

Good God my dear man the labor involved is a "magnum opus." I am only anxious to do another Forum if it can help the situation we are in—not complicate it. What we would do should be an asset to the Mag not a liability. My selfish interest is only to get something superior, if not extraordinary off my chest for the joy I could find in it and pride I could take in it. We've not much to gain by exploiting ourselves further—have we?

So, on the alert, we will keep getting together material that would be suitable for use; fine photographs of executed work; perfecting models and having an eye, while making plans, to make them good for reproduction.

When the time comes around for you let us know enough ahead and we will co-relate our efforts and go to it again. We shall have to abandon the plans we made for photo equipment and get a modest makeshift—which is all I ever had at my disposal in anything anyway until I got the new draughting room at Taliesin and until I finish this Desert Camp. Then I will have something to work with that you ought to see.

I always thought it was just around the corner but I will catch up with it, maybe, just as I have to quit.

Meantime my best to you, Howard. Use me when I can do something worth your while as an Editor with responsibility and an opportunity.

I'm coming to Boston the twenty-third and will try to see you. If I can't, as always with my best to Ruth and the boys.

> Affectionately as always,
> Frank

January 23, 1940

My dear Frank,

I have just come back from Minneapolis where it was 18° below, so I refuse to be chilled by letters from gentlemen who are philandering in the warming sunshine of Arizona.

As if we do not realize that the next Wright issue is a magnum opus. All I was trying to say is that it is also a magnum costus—one which, admittedly, adds enormously to our prestige but also one which, if we do it in the right way, is bound to add enormously to our deficit. Hence the necessity of our delaying such a work until we are in a better position to spend until it hurts. A further point is that we did hope the issue would be chiefly illustrated by photographs of completed work rather than with drawn plans—thereby gaining both clarity and conviction. Don't you agree?

I would tentatively like to think of this issue as something which might be synchronized with your Show at the Museum of Modern Art next Fall. That would give you enough time to do things in greater comfort and give us enough time to see how this year is going to look. If favorable, we could proceed on that schedule. If unfavorable, then I would only try to put it over until 1941. The prestige of the last Wright issue is far from spent.

Please do not read into this letter anything not intended. We are definitely going to do the issue, the only question being whether it will be this year or early next year. Since you are in higher favor with the Gods than am I, perhaps you will add your prayers to mine and maybe we can make the grade in 1940.

I am pleased that the Christmas package proved acceptable. Please convey my greetings to Mrs. Wright and to the Fellowship—and an affectionate salute to the Maestro.

Sincerely,
Howard

August 28, 1940

Dear Frank,

Doubtless you have long since catalogued me as an ingrate and scoundrel and to save unpleasant discussion, I will confess on both counts. The truth is I have been chasing around from State to State almost continuously since I put you on the train for Kansas City and this is honestly my first moment to write you.

There is no way I can tell you how much Mary enjoyed her stay with you. It was by all odds the great experience of her young life and was made the more memorable by Mrs. Wright's thoughtfulness, which set the pace for all the rest. "Little Myers" reminisces practically every hour on the hour and if and when you and Mrs. Wright agree that the time has come for her to join the Fellowship, there will be no holding Mary.

I have seen Ed Stone once and if you are not careful I am afraid you are also going to have him on your hands. I resent the fact that he has seen the Desert Camp before I have, but that has only doubled my determination to see it soon.

How are you progressing with the Frank Lloyd Wright issue No. 2 for January? What do you need to know from me, if anything? And should we really figure on January?

Louise and I were disappointed not to be able to make a longer stay but all in all I think the Myers family has done a pretty good job of imposing on your hospitality for the year of our Lord (which sometimes seems doubtful) 1940.

I am having a very handsome present made for you—at least it starts out to be handsome and if it turns out otherwise you will not see it. However, my affection for the gentleman who is to receive it is so great I am sure it will be a success. All I will tell you now is that it is smaller than a grand piano, larger than a brioche, does not bark but is guaranteed to be kind to its owner.

Howard

You can't guess what it is in a thousand years, so don't try.

September 2, 1940

Dear Howard:

Looks to me like now or never. January it is or nothing.

A big work looms ahead. A Radio City for Washington with changed conditions natural to Washington. We are heading in to it now but have a couple or three months before entire concentration must take place.

So let's go. I won't be interested in publicity after January next. As publicity goes thereafter the January Forum will be "swan song." So let's make it a good song.

We need only from you what help you can give. Say how many color plates we can have, how many pages are to be in the opus and how much money we can have for photographs as we would like to make them ourselves *right now*. Our facilities are ready. I mentioned $1,500.00 to you and got $500.00 which we will apply, etc., etc. The work will satisfy your exacting standards.

Kindly return the color shots of the Johnson Building I left with you. John McAndrew says he returned them to you and the drawing I left on your office wall, etc.

We all like Mary and she can have us when the time comes.

Our best to you all,
Affection—
Frank

September 14, 1940

Dear Frank,

Enclosed is a check for more money than I thought was left in the world. This $1,000 plus the $500 previously sent you, is to cover the cost of all photographs for the Frank Lloyd Wright No. 2 issue.

Next week I will forward some blank dummies should you wish to experiment with layouts. I hope you feel as I do that as many of the works as possible should be presented photographically as completed jobs. Naturally, we would likewise hope to include drawings of some other things now in process.

We are all delighted that the second volume is now under way.

Best to all,
Howard

MARCH 21, 1941
HOWARD L. MYERS

DEAR HOWARD:

THE DRAFT IS SERIOUSLY CUTTING INTO OUR WORK. COULD YOU HELP GET THE GROUP ON TO DEFENSE HOUSING, WITH CARMODY PERHAPS. THAT MIGHT KEEP OUR TRAINING BODY INTACT FOR THE TIME BEING. WE COULD DO A SWELL DEMOUNTABLE HOUSE JOB.

FRANK

MARCH 22, 1941

DEAR FRANK:

IN VIEW OF YOUR WIDELY PUBLICIZED OPINIONS, I WILL PROBABLY BE THROWN OUT OF MR. C'S OFFICE ON MY NOSE, WHICH DOESN'T MATTER AS IT IS LESS VALUABLE THAN YOURS. WILL MAKE THE ATTEMPT AND ADVISE YOU FROM WASHINGTON NEXT WEEK. GOD BLESS YOU AND KEEP YOU FROM EVER HAVING TO LIVE IN A DE-MOUNTABLE HOUSE.

                                    HOWARD

December 19, 1941

Dear Howard:

This is your Christmas—and extends to yours. If you can listen to Beethoven you can look at Hiroshige.

This print is a fine proof-copy something over a century old and an un-doubted masterpiece in graphic art. It is by no means common and should be kept protected as we have installed it for you. Your heirs and assigns may appreciate it more even than we do now.

                             With hope and affection—

December 30, 1941

Dear Frank—

What better than to look at Hiroshige—and think of you?

As he looks down on the world today I suspect that he would prefer to be with that other immortal at Taliesin than with his less inspired com-patriots in Tokyo.

My joy and pride in this gift are beyond the vocabulary of

                           your friend and admirer—
                           Howard

December 29, 1943

Dear Mr. Wright:

I am sorry you will be unable to be with us at the surprise luncheon
for Howard on January 4th, but I realize it was almost too much to hope
for.

When you send the telegram to Howard, would you be good enough
to address it to the office, marked for my attention, that morning?

With best wishes for the New Year, I remain

Cordially yours,
George P. Shutt

FEBRUARY 3, 1944

DEAR HOWARD:

TO HAVE BEEN AT YOUR SIDE TODAY WOULD HAVE GRATIFIED ME
NOT ONLY JUST FOR THAT BUT TO SAY THAT I THINK YOU ARE
AMERICAN ARCHITECTURE'S BEST AND WISEST FRIEND. IF YOU TAKE
1944 IN YOUR OWN STRIDE AND LIVE UP TO YOUR PAST YOU WILL
LIVE FOR THE FUTURE.

AFFECTION,
FRANK

August 9, 1945

Dear Frank:

Your comments which accompanied the copy of Arizona Highways
make me uncertain whether you approve or disapprove of this attempt
at color. In any event, we hope to do a great deal better in the next
Wright issue of the FORUM.

Last Sunday I had a great treat visiting the home of Lloyd Lewis and
spending a few hours with Mr. and Mrs. Lewis. They, like myself, were
dinner guests at Irving Florsheim's, who owns a farm across the River.

Much of the conversation naturally was about the Wrights. Sam and Florene Marx were also there. We had a truly grand time. Lloyd told an imperishable story about the occasion when the Auditorium was to be torn down, concluding with your comment, "This is the time when the truth is more important than the facts!" as of course it was.

Getting back to Issue No. 2 again, why don't we get Lloyd to do an introduction? You would probably appear with a clanking saber, dressed in the uniform of a Union general—not a bad picture at that.

Things are looking up, and we may have a larger size magazine and better paper around the first of the year. Then we can go to it.

Love to all.

Sincerely,
Howard

August 20, 1945

Dear Howard:

Don't be silly. No clanking militosis goes for me even by a best friend—even Lloyd.

No sir. The issue (if it ever issues) will be my Valedictory (the last will and testament to the boys) and no one can do that for me until the lid is screwed down.

But nothing written yet is what I want to use nor have we enough photographs of the right quality. Forget about Zevi's brochure. He writes me that there is already one English translation and the Italian publishers here commissioned him to go on with a book completely illustrated. He wants many photographs from me. I don't suppose they conflict in Italian, do they? So kindly return the small volume. Here's hoping your optimism can take it.

Perhaps moral quality and spiritual force evaporated with the profit motive supreme in a civilization.

Can't someone think of something better?

I hope your health stays good in all circumstances, Howard. Nothing else matters so much.

Affection,

I sent the "Highways" to show you that a brilliant mess can be made of perfectly superb material.

LIFE Magazine came to Taliesin West to interview and photograph Mr. Wright in the Spring of 1946. The article that appeared the following August came as a surprise to Mr. Wright when he walked into the drugstore of the little town of Spring Green, Wisconsin. He expressed his disappointment with the article in this letter to Howard Myers.

September 19, 1946

Dear Howard:

Your fine letter is good to see. If I lose your faith and friendship I lose too much to face at this latter end of a long day.

So far as the fast and Luce article in *Life* is concerned I had it in mind about right. I felt you could not have seen it. Six months expired after the first piece was prepared at Taliesin West and two months went by after you wrote me you had seen it. They must have rejected all the pictures their man Crane took of Fellowship activities and hastily borrowed a couple of Fortune's pictures for the rewrite. What caused the editorial swing I can't imagine....

In the *Life* piece there were eighteen direct mis-statements of fact all made with a malicious slant...

I was surprised by the return to the morgue by Winthrop Sargeant to get out an article dated about twenty one years ago. All since ignored for the desired affect. Whose desire? Why? Might be worth knowing.

We will sit down and talk it all over when I come down about mid October.

I enjoy seeing you and feeling that I am with a true friend as I always do with you. I haven't so many I enjoy.

I have reason to feel the affection for you that I do feel and this disagreeable episode isn't going to break into it.

Affection as always,

July 19, 1947

Dear Howard:

Your little secretary Dorothy was nice enough to tell me you are better. I have worried about you a lot and needed to know the good word.

Would have written as soon as I heard you were back in again but the trouble is: already too much of us and too many too often.

We (your friends) can't spare you to sickness. But we can't be greedy either when you are sick.

You are a hard case, Howard, but you will come through. Your love of life and your vitality is so great. Conserve your strength, man. Easy to say relax—be lazy—but I know how hard it is...

Affection,

SEPTEMBER 19, 1947
FRANK LLOYD WRIGHT
TALIESIN, SPRING GREEN, WISCONSIN

HOWARD PASSED AWAY LAST NIGHT. SERVICES SUNDAY AFTER-NOON, FOUR O'CLOCK.

LOUISE MYERS

TO HOWARD...

Just as The Forum of January 1938 was yours so this issue of January 1948 is yours. We were working on it together when I last saw you a day before you left and whatever this number of your magazine may mean is here dedicated to you. I saw no indication that you were going so soon, so had no chance and now have no need to say Goodbye. In truth I am unable to believe that you have gone—sure that what is you will see this work, as always, with the sympathetic and approving vision of an even greater spirit. We who loved the humor in your eyes and wit upon your tongue shall miss you but Architecture will not lose you. While fashion-ing a magazine for "profit" in equivocal times you steadily upheld the standards of Freedom and Truth. For a needy profession you greatly served despite its sense of itself.

A heart as deep as yours we see but seldom coupled with the fine discrimination you possessed or such loyalty to friendship.

Your helping hand reached this work some ten years ago at a time when something resembling neglect at home confronted it and you helped to change all that to something resembling appreciation. The end is not yet. You made The Forum on paper a Forum in fact. Your devotion to Architecture as a great Cause held true to its course as you steered your charge between the shoals of avarice and false-pride toward a more generous end.

And now young men in Architecture, everywhere, owe to Howard Myers more than to any journal or any school anywhere. They looked to what you were and did with brightened hope. They look upon you now with gratitude, sure of the sympathy and understanding that is as surely, love. To them you were and are the Future that is Now.

Frank Lloyd Wright
Taliesin

IV

60 YEARS OF LIVING ARCHITECTURE

In 1949 Arthur C. Kaufmann, cousin of Edgar Kaufmann, Sr., of Fallingwater, was in the office of Clare Boothe Luce, our Ambassador to Italy. They were discussing the rising tide of Communism in Italy since the end of World War II. One of the claims of Soviet propaganda was that America had no creed or culture beyond her worship of the dollar. To counter this propaganda, they came upon the idea of an exhibition of American art to show how living in a free country with freedom of expression could stimulate creative genius. They then inquired among Italian circles as to what the Italians themselves would most like to see from the United States. "Frank Lloyd Wright" was the unanimous reply. Even the Communist Mayor of Florence expressed enthusiasm for an exhibition of Mr. Wright's work.

Upon his return to the United States Mr. Kaufmann and his friend Oskar Stonorov, an architect from Philadelphia, met with Mr. Wright. Stonorov was engaged to take charge of the installation of the exhibit, first at Kaufmann's department store, Gimbel's, in Philadelphia, and then at the Palazzo Strozzi, in Florence.

Mr. Wright had a great affection for Italy, in particular for Florence where he had lived in 1909 while preparing drawings and text for the Berlin-published monograph on his work that appeared the following year and that had such impact upon the architects of Europe. The idea of Florence, as recipient of the exhibition, naturally appealed to him, and the text for the Italian catalog he took from the text of the Berlin monograph, which he himself had written in Florence in 1909, some 40 years before this current exhibit. The text was called "The Sovereignty of the Individual" and as well as presenting his work, it lauded the greatest moments of European culture, including the Florentine Renaissance and its two architects whom he admired, Brunelleschi and Bramante. As appropriate to the present as it was to 1909, the monograph defined creative endeavor as the product of the human soul.

The exhibition was entitled "Frank Lloyd Wright: 60 Years of Living Architecture." It was to be the largest architectural exhibition devoted to the work of one man that had ever been assembled. To prepare it occupied our autumn and early winter of 1950, when a full surge of activity took place in the Hillside drafting room at Taliesin. Departure for Arizona, the annual trek to the desert, was delayed this year in order to ready the material for the exhibition scheduled to open in Philadelphia in a few months. The weather turned cold, there was a light blanket of snow on the ground, and we stacked logs into the large fireplace at the north end of the drafting room and kept them burning day and night. Some drafting tables were moved to the side galleries so that the models could be brought out and worked upon. They were repaired, repainted, touched up. Mr. Wright selected new colors for them, adding and replenishing the always necessary "foliage," composed of sponge, pieces of balsa wood and glass beads, painted in shades of green for trees and foliage, and in bright colors to denote flower gardens.

The model of Broadacre City was cleaned, repaired and repainted to suit the new occasion. Mr. Wright explained to a group of us while looking at the model: "When we first built this model, at the Hacienda in Chandler, Arizona (1934) it was a city seen in midsummer. To portray this, the greens which we used on the blocks of wood for forests and planting were dark toned. Now we are about to open in Florence in May, and I would like this to be seen as a city in the fresh bloom of spring." We painted the foliage and forests light chartreuse, pale lavender, white, peach, soft rose, thus bringing all the fruit trees into bloom, producing long hedges of lilacs and spring blooming shrubs. The lakes and rivers were luscious blue, the roadbeds our own Taliesin red.

Many other models, some from the exhibition that had gone to Europe in 1931, others for the Museum of Modern Art show in 1932 and 1940, were selected and prepared, adding features or changing colors according to Mr. Wright's instructions. Photographs of constructed buildings were made to special large-size formats; over 800 original drawings covering his work from 1887 to 1950 were chosen for exhibition. Also of his own design were included furnishings, fabrics, flower-holders, stained glass windows. Assembled, crated, and sent to Philadelphia, the result of this massive work and energy was thus described by Gimbel's publicist:

Not since Michelangelo has the work of an architect had such profound influence on his contemporaries; and no other architect at the age of eighty-two has, since the days of the Renaissance, presented the world with the ever-increasing creative out-put of his work as Frank Lloyd Wright has done for the past sixty-three years.

Since the first publication of his "Buildings and Projects" in 1910 in Germany, the artistic world has been literally waiting for every new product of his fertile mind—his inventions in the field of building—his new conception of space—his many pieces of writing—his books—his philosophical treatises on American Democracy.

The exhibition tends to show the development of Wright's genius from 1887 to the present day. It represents a pictorial narrative not so much of details, but of the atmosphere of his buildings, of the scope of his projects, finished or conceived.

There is as much importance in the structures actually built as there is in the ideas of the buildings only dreamed about. The importance of Frank Lloyd Wright's work is as actual as it is posthumous. Wright's architecture is original in the very essence of the word, because structures as he built them have not existed before him. His houses are as sensitive to the needs of individual living as they are prophetic of methods to come. Wright's is today's architecture of tomorrow.

The exhibition of his work will contain a series of giant photographic views of the inside and outside of his buildings. There will be some twenty models of small and large houses, a theatre for Hartford, Connecticut; a Museum for New York; a skyscraper for San Francisco. There will be his famous model of his ideas on City Planning that he described in his book on "When Democracy Builds," a method of decentralized living: Broadacre City. Mr. Wright's voice will carry to the spectator his message of the significance of Broadacre City.

There will be a number of projects shown here for the first time. There will be a series of giant color projections of some of his most important buildings because his is an architecture in the nature of materials which includes color and the natural setting of the buildings on the land.

The exhibition will terminate with a full size section of a house that will convey to the visitor his architectural principles together with the feeling of Wright's space.

In addition to models, photographs and the full size house section, there will be a gallery of original drawings mostly by the master's hand—drawings from which those interested in the development of his *architecture will find the origin of many ideas current today...ideas that the average person would seldom connect with him.* The exhibition will occupy 10,000 square feet on the fifth floor of the Gimbel-Philadelphia Store.

Specific buildings and projects in the exhibition are models for: Guggenheim Museum, New York City; Skyscraper apartment, New York; Huntington Hartford Sports Club in Los Angeles; Skyscraper building, San Francisco; new theatre for Hartford, Connecticut and various private residences, including a large cut-away model of a small, three-bedroom house. Also, projects, for: the development of the Golden Triangle in Pittsburgh; a big spiral parking garage for Pittsburgh, and many others.

Among the projects and houses built are many small ones of very inexpensive construction designed for the needs of the average American family.

Wright has built in practically every State of the Union, and today, at the age of eighty-two, has approximately 130 building projects going all over the United States.

The show opened on schedule at Gimbel's in Philadelphia and then traveled to Florence for installation at the Palazzo Strozzi in May of 1951. Over 300,000 people had come to see it in Gimbel's alone, and in Italy Mr. Wright was accorded a ceremony of honor at the Doge's Palace in Venice as well as another in the Palazzo Vecchio in Florence. The exhibition was received with such enormous success and enthusiasm that it was requested by other cities in Europe. At this point, the American government agreed to sponsor the exhibition in its tour of other European countries and Mexico. From Italy it went to Switzerland under the auspices of Werner Moser and then to France, Germany and Holland. Across the Atlantic it traveled to Mexico. There, after being lost in shipment off the docks at Vera Cruz, it opened in Mexico City.

Returning to the United States, it opened in New York in 1953 and was set up in a specially designed pavilion on the vacant lot between 88th and 89th Streets on Fifth Avenue—the building site of the soon-to-be-constructed Solomon R. Guggenheim Museum.

In 1954 it traveled to Los Angeles and was installed in another specially constructed pavilion attached to Mr. Wright's famous Hollyhock House on Olive Hill. Finally it returned to Taliesin in Wisconsin, the models placed in the various galleries at Hillside, the photomurals on view throughout the building, and the drawings returned to the vault in our Arizona archives.

Although the exhibition was gloriously received wherever it went, so enormous an undertaking presented, with every move, problems involving freight, insurance, transport, space, catalogues, publicity, installation, demounting, and, by far not the least of them, money. Mr. Wright often found himself solely in charge of crises occurring thousands of miles away. The letters below reflect those problems as well as the acclaim and satisfaction he received from around the world.

November 9, 1949
Mr. Oskar Stonorov
Philadelphia, Pa.

Dear Oskar:

Truly I've forgotten to write Mr. Kaufmann of Gimbels. It was merely to say that I understood that the exhibition should be arranged by you to my entire satisfaction and exhibited in Italy under especial circumstances and conditions I could approve—and that all care should be taken to guarantee the safe return in specified time of all the material used in the exhibit and which either belonged or was to belong to us. This date and that of exhibition agreed upon.

As a preliminary: Mr. Kaufmann agreed to pay to the Frank Lloyd Wright Foundation, a cultural training ground in the Fine Arts, the sum of five thousand dollars in appreciation of the confidence reposed in him by this Foundation in sharing with him this extraordinary adventure in exhibition.

I am sending a copy of this to Mr. Kaufmann for confirmation and would be glad to see you here pretty soon as we take off for Arizona in about ten days.

February 15, 1950
Oskar Stonorov
Philadelphia, Pa.

Dear Oskar:

Believe me, I wasn't kidding. But I can look forward with pleasure to a show next fall, opening say Philadelphia in October; Florence in December and look forward to the first really comprehensive show—with your experienced cooperation in the whole business.

February 8, 1951
Mr. Oskar Stonorov
Philadelphia, Pa.

Dear Oskar:

Welcome when you care to come. Come in Station Wagon with family.

Send the drawings to Spring Green, attention of John Hill where they will be restored to the metal cases in their original position.

A note from Arthur K says he is after Museum of Modern Art to make movies of the show. I especially desire no connection with the M.M.A. as you know. So let's have movies owned jointly by the Architect (that's the Foundation) and the photographer who furnishes the prints: one copy to the Architect and other copies only to persons or places specified by the Architect. How about Jim Davis—30 Nassau Street, Princeton—he has made excellent films of both Taliesins. Plenty of operators would be interested on those partnership terms. In this way the fellowship boys could see the show for one thing. I thought a plane for sixty could be negotiated but A. K.—to whom I mentioned it—said trip would cost about $10,000.00. So we dropped it as out of scale.

No photostats of drawings yet. I guess affected by strike.

Weather lovely (right word) here.

I hope voice over Broadacres is only on once an hour. No obscene chairs around and the floor borders around models painted down to quiet them. Top edges of 2x4s might be left red if you think so.

I need specifications to communicate with those nations wanting the show. Kindly send. I think you should go to check up on installations but put in as separate item for consideration.

I am getting together two chairs for space model, early office chair, carpet, glass symphony and copper flower holders for the alcove as suggested long ago.

Let's try to keep publicity within bounds that are reasonable. If the dogs are turned loose on the quarry the thing will go to the bow-wows.

60 Years: entrance to the Exhibition

Mr. and Mrs. Frank Lloyd Wright, arrival in Italy

In Venice, with Count Sforza

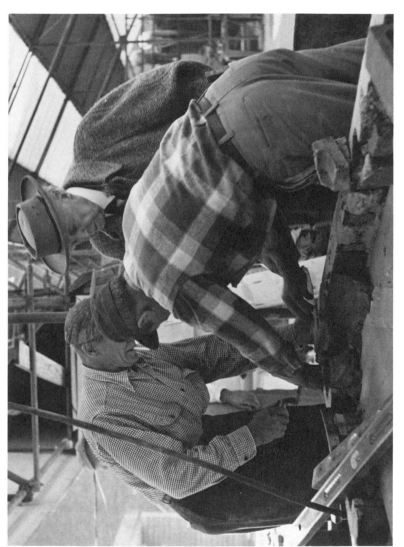
With workmen during construction of 60 Years site in New York City

DESCRIPTION OF THE EXHIBITION
OF THE LIFE WORK OF
FRANK LLOYD WRIGHT
AT
GIMBEL'S-PHILADELPHIA

The exhibition being assembled by Gimbel Brothers at the request of the City of Florence, Italy, and with the direct encouragement of the Italian Foreign Office and the United States Department, is the largest exhibition yet of his work. It is the first time that the American public will meet its greatest architect.

Mr. Arthur C. Kaufmann, Executive Head of Gimbel's, stated that the purpose of preparing this magnificent exhibition was (1) to bring a great creative mind before a large section of our people who have not yet seen his products; (2) to help cement among the free nations of the world the bonds of good will so much needed these days.

The exhibition will be shown at Gimbel's January 27th through February 25th, 1951.

After the event at Gimbel's, the material will be transported to Florence and erected in the historic Palazzo Strozzi, the office and living quarters of the merchant princes of the 15th Century now serving as a museum.

Official invitations have been received for its further showing at Zurich, Switzerland; London, England; Paris, France; Munich, Germany; Bombay, India and Stockholm, Sweden.

February, 1951
Bruno Zevi
Florence, Italy

Dear Bruno Zevi:

The Philadelphia preview has had an average attendance of about six thousand persons a day and is making a deep impression. I can't say how glad I feel that young Italy—youth of the nation that has given most in Architecture, Painting, and Music to the world—should now be seeking fresh hold on reality in Architecture (the Mother Art). Organic Architecture is that deeper way and in this exhibit if we can show the quality of the new life we all desire, no sacrifice will be too great, nor effort too much.

So, dear Zevi, let's do our very best to classify the ideal now becoming so dear to youth everywhere in the world and not allow it to be sidetracked further by the shallow dictums and staring facades of any "Internationalist Style." The terms of the exhibit, Stonorov is sending if not already sent.

I would like you to be arbiter of the installation in Italy—where it was designed to appear. Now it seems England wants the exhibit next—then Zurich—then Germany—then Paris—then home again. Other countries have requested it—Sweden, Finland, India, Denmark especially. But I am unwilling to go so long and so far with material we need here at home.

I hope all goes well with you in this poker playing world we all inhabit—sanity seems to have departed.

Let me know of anything I can especially do. A party of us (Mrs. Wright included) intend to fly over for the opening of the show in the Strozzi.

Meantime brotherly affection and faith—

February 28, 1951
Werner Moser
Zurich, Switzerland

Dear Werner:

Your experience in India seems disheartening but it all takes time and so patience. Sorry about Rana, too.

The exhibition—truly a great one—23 models, hundreds of drawings and hundreds of great blown up photographs is being packed for Italy—insurance, Lloyd's $100,000.00 requires 10,000 square feet. You will love it and I want Zurich to have it. Three weeks in each country (a week between) say Italy—opens May 15th—England—Switzerland—Germany—France—in that order. To be worked out.

Denmark, India, strangely, Finland and Sweden also want it but that takes too long away for our material needed here at home.

Will send you a diagram of the show at the Strozzi so you can arrange as you may. Sylva's Swiss Constitution came. Thanks to her.

The Swiss boys met a sad fate. They unfortunately entered as emigrants and to escape the draft have to get out of the country.

Affection,

March 2, 1951
Oskar Stonorov
Philadelphia, Pa.

Dear Oskar:

What you say about the mock-up is true all except that you had told me about it previously. The difficulties, yes. But when I saw the thing I thought you had solved them and the whole affair was collapsible and deportable. The first intimation I received otherwise was the drawing for the Strozzi showing it out.

Well, what now. I sat down to it yesterday and evolved a collapsible entirely of plywood like the screens you made (would like to know how much this stuff can be exported for)—furniture same. Put this frame up against the corner walls of the corner room displacing what you had there.

Looks good to me. Would like your opinion. We can manage this and furnishings too, I should think, by various contributions from those who might benefit from such display of their goods, etc., etc., etc.

Also I suggest a Sanctum for the craft pieces. I am now trying to get in my hands also books, drawings, etc., etc., near the entrance underguard.

Why don't you give yourself a vacation, put the family in the station wagon and we could work together on this and you could do the physiognomy as you intended. A week here should do it and benefit all concerned. This should be no later than March 20, I should say—if possible to you.

"a priori"—

March 7, 1951
Bruno Zevi
Florence, Italy

Dear Bruno:

The vexatious insurance matter has been settled and the splendid show is on the Atlantic bound for Italy. Stonorov has made layout which I send with some suggestions of my own for a full size mock-up of Usonian House proportions, etc., which was too big to transport entire. Drawings will follow. This can be set up or demounted easily and in the corner room of the Strozzi may be reasonably facsimile. What do you think.

Will you kindly let me know your reaction to the Stonorov layout.

I believe the Introduction to Ausgefuhrte Bauten translated into Italian would make an excellent opening letter from me as I am of the same feeling and opinion still. Use it if you want to do so and I will try to send another message though I am so desperately busy I am now on strict diet.

Meantime affection and hope—

April 30, 1951
Oskar Stonorov
Philadelphia, Pa.

Dear Oskar:

Don't be an old woman. Nobody called you names. In truth you are Kaufmann's agent as every architect is the owner's agent. Read the A.I.A. contracts. He employed you and paid you as far as that goes. Now I feel like this:

I gave my consent not to a Gimbel show but to an Italian show. I supposed A. K. in his Gimbel splendor was presenting Italy with the show. Not until we met at the Italian Ambassador's in Washington did it dawn on me that all was not well in that connection. But there was hope. I am sanguine. You only assumed I knew what was in your mind. Not until Gimbel's had its show did it become apparent to me that so far as Kaufmann (Gimbel's agent) was concerned, the show was over for him...when Gimbels closed.

The letters you quote as informing me were all post-show show-ups. I don't think you meant to put anything over on me. I think likely it was put over on you or was just sloppy technique. Nor did I undertand the appeal for contributions to copy all the drawings I entrusted to you. Then I was left to learn that the full-scale mock-up, so valuable a feature of the show, was for Gimbel's only.

Then, I did not know I had myself to pay the cost of getting the show to Italy by appeals for friendly money to get it across to them—by your good offices in my behalf.

Then I did not know you had to pay your way to set up the Italian show.

You see, I am naturally rather dumb, having come in from the country on a load of poles....

I also get it that now you want to help me set up the show I consented in the first place to give. But, you do it out of your own pocket which again lays me under financial obligation to you. I don't like you to pay out money to help me. I don't like to have you beg money to help me. I've been a very independent crab all these years but now, somehow, you say how I am no longer so. Your help was the condition upon which I consented to the show at Gimbel's. I regarded it steadily all the time as only preliminary to the real show—the one at the Strozzi....

So let's forget and start again.

I will be glad of your help in Italy and will somehow try to pay up for as much of it as I feel I should. As you say, I owe you the good fellowship gold medal for your prowess and your sacrifice. This for the brother act...

No show ever got a creative artist anything but the general use of his own stuff in competition with himself. I can't think of a single commission that ever came to me from any exhibition.

Well, I have added some things to the Strozzi show—probably the mock-up is out. I want to restore the Pittsburgh golden triangle to it. Don't yet know if the Irish model will be there. I've printed 2000 copies of an introduction to the show to be printed here at my expense and sent there for translation and distribution.

A letter from Zevi asks me to accept Italy's "ad honorem" from the State University of Venice—to go there to receive it. Nothing to do with the Strozzi. Apparently competitive. Paris, London, Zurich, Munich...all want the show. Also Cuba Libre and Brazil. I've written the general terms—suitable space, supervision of installation, proper share of insurance and transport—nothing else.

Have yet no commitments except Italian date. Perret is back of the Paris showing at the Beaux Arts; Jordan, director of the Art Association School of Britain and Robertson of the F.R.I.B.A. of the London event; Werner Moser at Zurich.

That is as far as I know now.

Cheer up, Oskar—we are not dead yet.

September 19, 1951
Bruno Zevi
Florence, Italy

My dear Bruno:

I was surprised to learn from Oskar that you had not received the note included with two prints (from my own collection) one for yourself and one for Mrs. Zevi. They were airmailed over six weeks ago, also prints to the Ragghianti's, the Scarpa's, the Samona's, and to Caracciolo, Palermo (including a fine one—the eagle and the cask—to the little pupils he brought with him to see me at the Excelsior).

We are trying to trace them from this end but you could do better from your end, I believe. Please try. They are all too valuable to be lost.

I have given Edgar K., Jr. something else to edit, so you are free to do the book as you wished. The Autobiography I have scanned and noted changes in wording that ought to make it easier to translate and to read. They will be incorporated in the next edition by Duell, Sloan and Pearce, the present publishers.

The copyright is in my name. So I give you full authority for Italian translation.

I am still charmed by the warmth and intelligence of our Italian experience—especially Venice. We look forward to someday having you all here at Taliesin for a good time. Italy gave me the feeling that I had "come home" at last.

There is no building I have done that would not be gracious in Medieval Italy. So it seems.

My love to you all and especially to your charming wife. There must be great times ahead for us all if we can stem the present tide of the old materialistic mistakes being made new all over the Earth.

With deepening affection,

December 18, 1951
Oskar Stonorov
Florence, Italy

Dear Oskar:

Speaking of the strange and incomprehensible—you seem to take the cake. Since Christmas is so near, let's hope it is a fruit cake.

From you I've had no explanation of the fluke in France. I heard you were in Naples when you were expected in Florence. I've had no explanation of the loss of the congratulatory gifts I sent to our friends in Florence and in Venice—which I hoped you would clear up.

You fly here, there and everywhere and confusion, delay and uncertainty seems to follow in your wake. I hear about shirts, etc.

In simple French, Oskar, "What the hell"?

Am I entitled to some clear and responsible statement of these mysterious delays where my investment in Architecture entrusted to this "show" is concerned? Your ample fanny sits on the facts if indeed you really do know what is happening. If you don't, kindly say so. If you do know, kindly let me in on what so *vitally* concerns me. Will you?

January 28, 1952
Werner Moser
Zurich, Switzerland

ZURICH is Switzerland to me and The United States of Switzerland is the perfect pattern for The United States of Europe.

May the honor of Switzerland's heroism, amidst the most brutal family brawl in all history, never diminish. From its premier in the Strozzi Palace at Florence this adequate collection of my work comes to Zurich for exhibition. Italy is still the beating heart of the creative-art world. Astonished, I saw that not one modern work included in the exhibition but would have graced Medieval Italy as against the Renaissance. I am glad this event takes place in Zurich in the museum built by Professor Karl Moser, one of that distinguished group of European architects to which Berlage and Otto Wagner belonged and brought the architectural thought of Europe abreast that of Louis Sullivan in my own country. Your Congress House is worthy continuation of that early devotion to a great ideal.

I have twice experienced the loveliness, love and hospitality of Zurich. With gratitude by this exhibition I hope for the third time to help point the path of progress toward a free architecture fit for the youth of your country. A free architecture for a free people is only free so long as maintained on a basis of principle. This is the message this exhibition brings with love and hope from the United States of America to the young architects of the United States of Switzerland.

March 20, 1952
Joseph Samona
Venice, Italy

My dear Joseph Samona:

A competent English translation of your extraordinary criticism of my work has just reached me. I have enjoyed for the first time in my life comprehensive insight of the nature of that work.

Few indeed are the exceptions I would take to what you said, always admiring the way you said it. A minor point might be your reference to European influence in the case of Fallingwater. I think you will find the original of this house in the wood and plaster Gale house in Oak Park built 1907. The change in grammar came naturally with the first use of steel reinforced concrete which had never been given to me before in my residence work. The rounded horizontal edges of all planes entirely removing the treatment of the material from European resembles which by that time were coming my way.

Again as to other general or specific influences—all were and still are more resemblances due to the use of principle wherein results resemble the instinct of primitives than anything conscious in my use of their instincts. Congratulations on your insight.

Incidentally, Aalto's work on M.I.T. affects me as inspirational as a clumsy grub. No chrysalis is that Dormitory of his. But I like him.

I want you all to know that when we returned home I went into my collection of antique Japanese prints, picked out one for each of my Italian friends and their wives—eight in all—sent them in care of Ragghianti care Palazzo Strozzi and have just learned (nearly a year later) that they were confiscated by the Italian Government. How to trace them now is the question.

We have the warmest affection and gratitude for our Italian friends especially the Venetians and look forward to having you all over here with us for a holiday.

Meantime our very best to Mrs. Samona and your good self. The Italian experience was a rich one to stay with us a lifetime.

April, 1952

MESSAGE TO FRANCE

In a frightened world lost to soul by way of Force, O France, you have had a substitute for soul. Your substitute is delicacy. Do not lose the grace of your touch. Do not be misled by a frightened people that count on its fingers freedoms up to four because they do not know Freedom.

Freedom's secret is within the Spirit and, notwithstanding Napoleon, the lustre of France does not lie in the harsh glare of militarism but lives in her own genius—the love of reason in her philosophers and the love of beauty in her poets. France really lived when she lined up on the side of Freedom, Equality, and Fraternity: a lesson learned from the forefathers of the United States of America but which those States now seem to be in danger of forgetting.

O France, put your trust in your native genius. Internationalism is good only when and where preserving what is French in France, Italian in Italy, British in Britain, Russian in Russia and it consists in appreciation by each and every Nation of what constitutes the soul of the other and insists upon uniting for the protection of that Individuality.

I bring to France Architecture Free—free because based upon organic Principles. Free because of infinite variety found in the truth that Form and Function are one. Organic Architecture free of academic Tradition, free of all Tradition except Principle, is the greatest discipline as well as the greatest inspiration on earth. Because it is voluntary and interior Organic Architecture is the sovereign Architecture of Democracy.

"Free" means unafraid, self confident because sure of its ground and its star—fully aware of the fact that the soul of one race has not the color or precise form of any other but all have the love of truth in common and Truth is found by knowing Principle, knowing that Form and Function are one, that Beauty either of character, Form or Facade must be wooed and won by love alone.

Unity in variety is in the mind of the Creator. When one species becomes too dominant it is destroyed. Beauty can never yield to Force.

Frank Lloyd Wright
Taliesin West

May 1, 1952
Mr. Philip C. Johnson
Museum of Modern Art, New York City, N.Y.

Dear Phil:

You should see the Beaux Arts now!
I'll see what the Museum people have to say about the show for their outfit.
So far as I'm concerned—fine.
And thanks for the photos Albert sent to Munich.

Affection,

May 1, 1952

TO GERMANY

To two great but various cultures I owe most in that strange occurrence we call our education: to Old Germany and Old Japan. Both are no more except as they are alive and working in the soul of all humanity today.

I am happy to say they are living in mine. Both were working in what you will see of this exhibition of a large portion of my life-work as an architect.

Goethe, Beethoven and Nietzsche, their inspiration has lasted me lifelong, I knew so many other great Germans. With me also were the great Japanese, Rikyu, Sesshu and "moderns" like Korin, Sotatsu, Hiroshige and Hokusai. A multitude of great artist craftsmen I learned to know when working upon the Imperial Hotel in Japan from 1913 to 1919. Their inspiration is mine to this day. They went to school to Germany but went the wrong way.

German culture was more nearly ready for Organic-architecture in my early life as an architect than my own people in our United States. Kuno Francke, exchange professor of aesthetics at Harvard came to Oak Park, Chicago, to see my buildings in the Spring of 1909. Delighted by what he saw, he then and there tried to persuade me to come to Germany because he said my people were not ready for me but the German people were. Returning to Germany, soon afterward, he instigated the publication of my work by Wasmuth, 1910, Berlin: the "Ausgeführte Bauten and Entwürfe."

Also, (but later) the Japanese sent a commission around the world to find an architect for the new Imperial Hotel. They first heard of me in Germany, and came straight to see my buildings. They said: "Nothing Japanese about these buildings, but would look well in Japan." They employed me to come and build the Emperor's new clearing-house for the foreign social obligations incurred by official Japan.

Somehow the two cultures—German and Japanese—came together in my life to enable me to further the education I had begun with both.

Gratitude is mine. I hope to see Germany, the great outpost of Western Culture, divested of the old militarist complex which somehow I had never realized was so German as it seemed to become. What was profound in great German culture is inevitably now in the life-blood of the Western World for great good; probably the most valuable strain in it. What would Western Culture be without it?

The profound in Old German Culture must come back to us all again. I have never doubted but it would come strengthened and purified by the agony of defeat. No physical destruction can destroy the indomitable German love of beauty in the Song that is Life.

She will build her love into a great Architecture, greatest of Arts—now the blind-spot of the world and take her rightful leadership where she belongs—in the growing realm of Democratic Nations.

Old Germany has been and is still my love, never faltering and a great hope. She will suffer, but will never be destroyed.

Frank Lloyd Wright
Taliesin

May 15, 1952
To the Minister of the Ecole des Beaux Arts
Paris, France

Honored Sir:

It is my distingished privilege to thank you and your officials one and all for the remarkable manifestation of hospitality extended to my work and to me in the recent exhibition in the great halls of the Ecole in Paris.

It has been my wish—always—that the friendship between our nations hitherto so close in politics, should continue and grow in our culture.

I have been assured by many in both France and the United States that this affair at the Beaux Arts has contributed greatly to that much desired end.

Therefore, my dear sir, I assure you of my satisfaction in this display of friendship, so far as I could see, on the part of everyone concerned.

May the Cause of a free architecture continue to grow and look back with gratitude upon this auspicious occasion.

Faithfully, my dear sir, with a wish to be kindly remembered to all of you who had a share in establishing the event—

I am most truly yours,

June 1, 1952

TO HOLLAND

Long ago this work owed appreciation to Holland when understanding of the nature of the work was not only new but rare.

Visiting America, the eminent Dutch Architect Berlage raised his voice in praise. Said he, "The two things which impressed me most in the United States were Niagara Falls and the Larkin Building." Architect Oud wrote in: "De Styl" an article which reached and encouraged me while I was unfortunate. Then Widjeveld and Wendingen came through with one of the most splendid of the many publications devoted to my effort in the direction of a native creative-culture. This publication reached me at a time when I was walking the streets of New York getting a worm's eye view of society.

Exhibitions of this work have known Holland before.

One, I remember, under Widjeveld at Amsterdam 1930. The American Ambassador, asked by Widjeveld to open the show, said, "Who is this man Wright anyway." The Ambassador came, waved the American flag. But Widjeveld made the Ambassador's speech.

As an architect I have had occasion to admire the work of Architects Oud, Dudock, Widjeveld and other Dutchmen. A young Dutch patriot Can T. Hoff made his appearance in Chicago very early in my day and took home something of what he then saw there on the Chicago prairie.

At that same trying time in my life my first academic honor came to me from the Academic Royale D'Anvers, no doubt influenced by my Dutch friends, nearby. So I felt at home in Holland when again it was so happening in this world that a native culture dawning in a new nation was not recognized by its own provincials before that dawning had been noticed and approved in Europe where most of the people of the new nation came from.

So Holland will always have a warm place in my heart and due respect from my head.

My greatest admiration for her cultural achievements.

They establish Holland as one of the fundamental assets in world-culture by which what is vital in Art today stands up nobly under the test of time.

One of the truly independent Democracies on earth, she has suffered and shared much that is to be the soul of the new world-order. Someday common to us all.

I cannot imagine her contribution in any and every cultural field left out of the eventual reckoning.

Architecture is basic to that field.

More and more comes the recognition that the principles of Organic Architecture lie in the core of the freedom that we call Democracy.

So how glad I am to again know that there on exhibition in Holland is what I have for a lifetime done in that direction, sure that there is the kind of home-coming I would wish I might myself see and talk with you Hollanders about the great cause nearest our hearts today: world-peace. Organic peace can only come when the great Principles of the Art of Architecture organic are really understood. If they were they would soon be established as basic to the society and politics of this world.

So to you—mightly little nation—so right and so strong in the continuity that is the Future, this "The Italian Exhibition" is a friendly visitor already known to you. Of your welcome I feel assured because your feeling for truth and beauty has never yet failed you as a nation nor will ever fail humanity.

Frank Lloyd Wright
Taliesin

June 13, 1952
Oskar Stonorov
Philadelphia, Pa.

Dear Oskar:

By circumstantial evidence I owe your account of the Munich affair to the fact that I hold the return half of three round trip tickets to Paris—which I propose to either get extended as returning or going over again, say within the year.

But you do not mention this. I should like Pan Am tickets exchanged for TWA also. I feel that Pan Am is the meanest of all the Transport lines. Well—anyway, Oskar is back again with a good account of a well-staged exhibition No. 5!

I have seen no Munich catalogue, have heard nothing. I suppose they considered it good enough to let you do it—as you were present.

Concerning further exhibitions, I think we have had enough—unless we stage one at the Metropolitan in New York City on the return of the show from Rotterdam.

I must say I do not understand the cause for these perpetual financial difficulties you have wallowed in unless the people we are dealing with are fundamentally dishonest from first to last.

Everywhere you go there is financial pain and loss. Perhaps eventual ruin? Is this the fate of every show-man more or less? Or what is it? Art?

Perhaps Art is (like Religion) something one gets for nothing. Comes cheap. The age we live in doesn't recognize it is essential. But you wanted to go to Munich and I thought it was your turn to go. Not at your own expense. That they should correct.

I knew they couldn't afford to pay for self and Olgivanna and you would be more useful. So it was up to you instead of us. Will write Miss D'Ortschy when I hear from her. Glad too that Roland and Maresia did well. Have you rewarded Brigitte? Have you a suggestion? Should I send her money?

As for citation etc., Germany gave me her highest many years ago when her head was up and she was a going institution. We honor her in this case.

I imagine you will always witness the lethargy of management if it can depend on your performing the task.

Ezra is still bitter as hell. Offered to bet me over a thousand dollars you would come out of this with more than I would, etc., etc. Probably we should get his bill paid by some combination of beneficiaries. Name them!

Portraits, Oskar, do not appeal to me. I think I am too many people ever to be put into one presentment. Anyway they all give me pain. I am that pain—I don't think my vanity so dense as yours, Oskar, but it serves.

Will be seeing you at the A.I.A. Convention in New York where you will be telling all your troubles. Better to tell of your triumphs. No one likes to hear from the maiden how much she suffered when she lost her maidenhead...but they like to hear of her ectasy?

Be good now, Oskar, till I see you.

> Affection—and to your wonderful lit-
> tle family!

July 3, 1952
Frank Lloyd Wright
Taliesin, Spring Green, Wisconsin

Dear Master and Friend Frank Lloyd Wright,

Yesterday we opened your exhibition and I delivered a short speech. I think you can be satisfied. Like you requested me, I supervised the whole thing. I looked for a good man to design the posters, the folders and the catalogue, and for making the arrangement of the material (Mr. Wissing). I have studied everything with him and I have suggested that the exhibition should be arranged less dull than in Paris: it should be more lively and attractive for a broader public. For that reason there is a little waterpool (with a-working-fountain) in the hall; there are a lot of beautiful flowers, plants, cactus, a bit of rock-parties a.s.o. At the end of the hall there is some part of living nature by *two parrots*. No don't be afraid: it does not at all look like "kitsch" but it gives the whole show a bit of the atmosphere that your houses must have in reality.

Furthermore: postage-stamps coming from Rotterdam are stamped with "Frank Lloyd Wright-tentoonstelling"; carriages of the tram have little flags with indication of your exhibition too. We sent a lot of folders to everywhere in Holland and in the neighbour-countries. I held a press-conference for the exhibition. Rotterdam is a fine town and the best people in Rotterdam do their best to make your exhibition a success. The American Ambassador opened it.

To finish: you suggested in Paris that I could earn the money which now need not be paid to Stonorov. I like you to know that I did not take one cent from the exhibition for it, because I like to do it for you and for your work.

Our best greetings to you and your wife,

Affection

Your Oud

Yes: you can do one thing for me. I am much interested in your book "Genius and the Mobocracy" but I cannot get it here. Please send me a copy and write some nice words in it!

September 19, 1952
Mr. Frank Lloyd Wright
Taliesin, Spring Green, Wisconsin

Dear Mr. Wright:

On my return from Europe this week I was delighted to find the copy of the catalogue of the exhibition at the Ecole des Beaux-Arts in Paris. I have been fortunate enough to catch the exhibition in Rotterdam and (I hope with your approval) have all summer been doing everything I could to see that the exhibition should be shown this fall in London. I believe that, in part as a result of my activities, a proper place is now being found for the exhibition; namely, the foyer of the Royal Festival Hall, whose architects Robert Matthew and Leslie Martin are most anxious that the London County Council should provide this space. There is also a problem of finances, and I am awaiting definite word that the space at the Festival Hall is available and precisely what sum of money is needed before I start to write various people who I hope will be willing to contribute toward the rather considerable sum which will apparently be needed.

Putting off my sailing by nearly two weeks has left me with no time to come to Taliesin before college opens. I hope, however, that you will be coming East shortly and that you will let me know so that we may get together in New York with Duell to discuss a new edition of "In the Nature." [his encomiastic study of Mr. Wright's work]

I had a pleasant evening with your admirer, Mr. Zevi, in Rome who kindly showed me a lot of the new work there. I can't say much for it, least of all perhaps for Zevi's own work. But he is a most energetic character and doubtless a better writer and teacher than he is architect.

The European architectural scene in these post-war years seems pretty thin. I can only hope that the sight of your work in the exhibition which has travelled so broadly may stimulate a new cycle of activity. Only in LeCorbusier's block of apartments at Marseilles and in certain English work did I find much vigor. But on the whole, it would seem that the U.S. now leads the world in architecture.

Yours sincerely,
Russell

September 24, 1952
Henry-Russell Hitchcock
Smith College Museum of Art
Northampton, Massachusetts

Dear Russell:

Yes—at bottom it always has. But who knew where the bottom was? We will get together next time in New York. Can't say just when now but will let you know. Will discuss publication matter then with you and Charles—the Duell, etc.

Affection and hope,

August 30, 1952
Carlos Lazo, Presidente
Colegio Nacional De Arquitectura, Mexico City

My dear Architect Lazo:

I should be happy to accept Mexico's kind invitation to come with Mrs. Wright to attend your convention next October. Also I am enclosing the catalogues of the Beaux Arts Paris and the Rotterdam shows—so you may see the scope of the exhibition which I propose to send from Rotterdam to Mexico City for the fortnight of your convention week if your society so elects.

Ten thousand square feet will be required in some appropriate place—with proper insurance for the time it is in responsible keep there. We will bear the cost of landing the exhibition weighing thirty thousand pounds at Vera Cruz if your society will transport it safely to the place of exhibition in Mexico City and furnish adequate assistance to unpack and set it up and pack it again for transport by truck to Taliesin, Spring Green, Wisconsin where it is to be permanently installed.

In Venice, Zurich, Paris, Florence, and Rotterdam $10,000.00 was required besides 10,000 sq. feet of space in the most important gallery in town. But I am undertaking (with the help of several of my friends) to take over the financial burden involved if Mexico will stand under the above mentioned items to the best of her ability.

The exhibition is large—comprehensive—and of course very valuable (but it is insured for $100,000.00 only to make exhibition easy).

So I should want your assurance that every possible protection and aid would be forthcoming if the collection of 23 models, 800 original drawings, and nearly 100 "blowups," 8'0 x 8'0, were entrusted to you for exhibition at Mexico City on the occasion of your Congress.

Mr. Edgar Kaufmann from our country would assist and Mr. Oskar Stonorov, who designed the installation, would come down to put all in proper order—with such help as your society could render.

If this is agreeable to your society will you notify me at once as the exhibition is now in Rotterdam and the time is getting short.

October 1, 1952

SALUDOS AMIGOS

This comprehensive exposition of my work is routed from Europe by way of Mexico City instead of London because our companion-nation of the South seems to me, just now, to be more in need of inspiration. This work may have something to offer Mexico in the new direction of Architecture Free in Mexico to be itself Mexican, eventually—say in a quarter of a century—a true expression of the individual humanity that is Mexico, the great Primitive, instead of the standardized typewriter Architecture evolved from European modern now so much in evidence there. Much of it is the expression of a mental-confusion and spiritual poverty. Mexico deserves a richer share in the struggle to advance the great culture that is Organic in Architecture.

To most North Americans Mexico has become the great Nation of contradictions. She is the great Primitive struggling now to resolve these contradictions. This greatly favored and most beautiful land of magnificent historical Romance is worthy of a great Architecture. So the gospel of an Organic Architecture is the true basis as well as the heart of appropriate culture for the beauty-loving Mexicans. Thus it seems to me that what I have done is needed here while my confreres are concentrated at the eighth Pan American Conference.

I hope this conclusion will meet with approval and the characteristic enthusiasm of the Mexican nature. Should my confreres, whom I greatly esteem, approve I shall be happy and consider the show, as well as myself, well spent.

My best to my Mexican comrades—in true friendship.

Frank Lloyd Wright
Taliesin

November 15, 1952
Carlos Lazo, Presidente
Colegio Nacional De Arquitectura, Mexico City

My dear Lazo:

Greetings and congratulations to you and your brave band of architects. The Congress was a remarkable example of American progress and brotherhood. Out of it something great for the future is sure to come.

You must be proud of your share in the whole affair and I hope my contribution added to the world-significance of the great occasion, which was really a great re-union. I enjoyed meeting my fellow American Architects and am more than ever sure that American Architecture needs only American influences originating in the Toltec area as the great basis of all future Architecture if we are to carry on to a great life of our own in our own time.

Swiss or French influence is now behind the American lighthouse and I hope it stays there. It is all that is the matter with American Architecture today and now stands in our way.

I have been at Cornell University, Ithaca and the University of Wisconsin extolling the Mexican performance and urging our own people to wake up and take a great lesson from Mexico City.

I hope the "big show" of my own American Architecture did some good service to the cause of Architecture in the Americas.

In our country they are arranging to put it on at the Metropolitan in New York sometime in December. Date not yet fixed. If it is not in your way down there I would like to leave it under Mexican protection until the twenty fourth of November when someone will come down to help get it properly packed for shipment to New York. Perhaps by sea?

You were so busy when we left I didn't want to bother you to say goodbye. Daughter Iovanna had been taken very sick (now all right again) so I paid my score at the hotel and our own fares back home again.

I have received from the Congress only a one way passage for myself to Mexico City. So if the Congress is inclined to keep the arrangement to transport Mrs. Wright and myself from Spring Green, Wisconsin to Mexico City, keep us there for a week and return to Wisconsin—you may figure that out at what was expected. We should have only the usual allotment. You know what that is. I do not.

In any case we feel very close to you all and will do whatever lies in our power to promote the cause of American culture in your part of our

Continent. Remember us kindly to the Marescals. They are a great family and to Santacilia especially. Our affection and thanks to yourself and your very handsome wife. Sometime you are coming to America to visit us we hope.

V

THE R.I.B.A. AND THE A.I.A.

On December 29, 1940 His Majesty King George VI of England instructed that the following letter be sent to Frank Lloyd Wright from Windsor Castle:

"The King has been pleased to approve that
Mr. FRANK LLOYD WRIGHT
should be His Majesty's Gold Medalist of the Royal Institute of
British Architects, for the year 1941.
The Medal will be presented after the war."

Two nights later, sitting in the garden room at Taliesin West on the Arizona desert, Mr. and Mrs. Wright and their Taliesin Fellowship heard the above announcement over the radio that would arrive by mail within a few days. Mr. Wright was deeply touched that England, a nation beleaguered and embroiled in a world war, would still be able to look across the ocean and give its highest honor in architecture to an American citizen from the prairies of the Midwest.

Mr. Wright had been in England the previous year to deliver a series of lectures at the Sulgrave Manor Board, where he occupied the Sir George Watson Chair. These four lectures were supplemented by films shown of his work, including the Johnson Building and Fallingwater in construction, Taliesin West in construction, and the Fellowship at work both in Arizona and Wisconsin. He enjoyed the British audience enormously, said that they were the best to whom he had ever lectured because they asked pointed questions, got into heated arguments amongst themselves during the course of asking their questions, and kept the evening sparkling with their enthusiasm and keen perception. The lectures he delivered were then compiled into a book entitled, *An Organic Architecture*, published in London and illustrated with photographs of his then recent work.

The Royal Gold Medal was not the first of the world-wide honors that had come to Mr. Wright, nor by far the last. In fact, they continued to arrive at an increasing rate all during his lifetime. By the year 1948 he had received the following honorary citiations and awards:

Kenchiko Ho: Royal Household, Japan Conferred by the Imperial Household represented by Baron Okura	1919
Honorary Member: Academie Royale des Beaux Arts, Belgium Conferred by the State	1927
Honorary Member: National Academy of Cuba Conferred by the State	1927
Extraordinary Honorary Member: The Akademie der Kunst (Royal Academy), Berlin Conferred by the Reich	1929
Honorary Member: National Academy of Brazil	1932
The Sir George Watson Chair: The Royal Institute of British Architects Academic honor by the Sulgrave Manor Board	1941
The Royal Gold Medal for Architecture The Royal Institute of British Architects Conferred by King George VI	1941
Honorary Member: National Academy of Architects Uruguay	1942
Honorary Member: National Academy of Architects of Mexico Conferred by the State	1943

Honorary Member: The National Academy of Finland   1946
Conferred by the State

Citations, medals, honors, and awards came to him from all over the world—from Finland, Mexico, Brazil, Germany, Cuba, Uruguay, Japan, Belgium, Holland, England; honors even from his grandfather's ancestral Wales. But the leading architectural organization in his own country, the American Institute of Architects, ignored him until on April 19, 1948, Mr. Arthur Holden wrote to him: "I know that you would accept an award [the A.I.A. Gold Medal] if it represented impulses you believed were fine."

Mr. Wright replied: "I am no cad and would never refuse a token of friendship and esteem sincerely tended even as an 'honor.'"

On March 17, 1949, at the Rice Hotel in Houston, Texas, Mr. Wright accepted the Gold Medal of the American Institute of Architects.

The letters in this final section chiefly concern the Royal Institute of British Architects and the American Institute of Architects and the honors and medals awarded to Mr. Wright. But their deeper theme is the vindication of his architectural principles. His speech in acceptance of the A.I.A. Gold Medal proclaims his lifelong work in the cause of Organic Architecture and reiterates his adherence to Principle and his fundamental faith in Democracy.

November 4, 1940
Frank Lloyd Wright
Taliesin, Spring Green, Wisconsin

Mr dear Mr. Lloyd Wright:

It is with the very greatest pleasure that I have to announce to you that the Council of the Royal Institute of British Architects have decided to recommend to his Majesty the King that the Royal Gold Medal for Architecture for 1941 should be awarded to you. This decision is for the moment of a confidential nature because we have to get the formal approval of the King before any public announcement is made.

May I have the great pleasure of telling my Council that you are prepared to accept the Royal Gold Medal for which you have been nominated?

I enclose a copy of our last Kalendar 1939/1940. You will find on page 16 of it a complete roll of the Royal Gold Medalists from 1848 down to 1939. It is a remarkably interesting and varied list and, as you will see, it contains the names of thirty one non-British architects from Europe and America. We have had three from the United States and their names are an interesting comment on current ideas and tastes: in 1893 Ric. Morris Hunt, 1903 Chas. F. McKim, in 1922 Thomas Hastings.

One of the most interesting names of all is not on the list for a peculiar reason. Fifty or sixty years ago the medal was offered to John Ruskin. He refused it, not because he was not greatly impressed by the compliment, but because he had just received news that the Italian Government had destroyed a beautiful old building in Northern Italy. He said that at such a time all architects and people interested in architecture ought to be sitting in sackcloth and ashes and mourning their failure to prevent an act of vandalism rather than awarding Gold Medals to one another.

I hope that in spite of all the trouble of the time you are keeping well and Taliesin is flourishing.

With kindest regards,

Yours very sincerely,
Ian MacAlister, Secretary
Royal Institute of British Architects

December 31, 1940
Frank Lloyd Wright
Taliesin, Spring Green, Wisconsin

My dear Mr. Lloyd Wright,

Royal Gold Medal, 1941.

It was a great pleasure to get your cable of the 17th instant and to know that you are prepared to accept the honour and I shall let my Council know at their next meeting. His Majesty the King has formally approved the award and a public announcement of the fact is now being made.

Believe me,
Yours very sincerely,
Ian MacAlister

January 1, 1941
Mr. Frank Lloyd Wright
Taliesin, Spring Green, Wisconsin

Dear Frank Lloyd Wright,

The best news we have had for a long time was in the evening papers to-day and on the radio news at 6 o'clock this evening, and it was that His Majesty the King had approved the award of the Gold Medal of the Royal Institute of British Architects to Frank Lloyd Wright. All of us who admire your work and everything you stand for in architecture, feel that this recognition is not only just, but overdue. It has at last been recognised that the greatest living architect belongs to the English speaking peoples: it is too late to-night to send you a cable, but one will be sent to you to-morrow to express the tremendous personal pleasure it has given to the whole Gloag family.

With kindest regards to yourself and Mrs. Wright,

Sincerely yours,
John Gloag

January 22, 1945
Talmadge A. Hughes, The American Institute of Architects
Detroit, Michigan

My dear man:

You put me up against the same old hard-spot! Forty years past I've had to seem uncooperative and ungracious by refusing to join the Institute. Perhaps I can make clear to you why I refuse again.

I do not join the A.I.A. because I am more interested in Architecture than in the Profession and I felt, as I still feel, able to serve not only Architecture but the Profession better outside the Institute than in it.

I crave good-will and the comradeship of my kind—every man does. But I've felt that I couldn't do the work I wanted to do inside any "Profession." I've had to be a free-lancer and become anathema to the good old guard: the A.I.A. As I then felt, I still believe that Architecture (my real objective) is more than ever Discipline in deciding this matter.

I believe no man can really cooperate except as he maintains the independence of his Spirit. If he becomes interdependent, he is gone, in the same way that (so it seems to me) our National Democracy is gone. But I have never refused anything the boys ever asked of me when I could render it on decent terms.

The Profession is in reality more Personal than Principle. Besides this, I know my own limitations in the personal way. Principle makes bad fellows of us all when we come against the hard choice between good-fellowship and the interior discipline of Principle.

There is enough to struggle with when all is fine. Imagine then how much the strain is multiplied by intimate association with congenital opposition or inordinate comradeship.

Does this seem to you as though I consider myself superior to my fellows in the Profession? If so, you are wrong. I frequently envy some of them and wish it all were for me as it seems to be for them. Not that I would trade places—or, even now, regret the isolation that seems to have chosen me.

What I have, what I have done and what I am belongs to my fellows whether either I or they like it or not. But, my dear Talmadge, I want what I have given and what I still have to give to be unhampered by personal or professional considerations.

I hope you won't misunderstand and resent.

Faithfully yours,

July 21, 1947
Mr. C. D. Spragg
Secretary of the Royal Institute of British Architects
London, England

Dear Secretary Spragg:

The Royal Gold Medal has arrived and duly admired.

I thank my British brothers from the bottom of my heart. In case they should find it expedient or essential to print another photograph of me at any time I am sending one by Karsh—a little nearer the truth. I hope.

April 19, 1948
Mr. Frank Lloyd Wright
Taliesin West, Phoenix, Arizona

Dear Frank:

Two years ago Ralph Walker started an agitation in the Institute of Architects over the failure to recognize your achievements. He stood up in one of the conventions and said that the A.I.A. had followed the policy of waiting until after its great men died to award them the Gold Medal, and he cited a long list of posthumous awards. He then made a motion that only a limited number of posthumous awards be permitted.

This year Henry Churchill has actively taken up the campaign. He wrote a series of letters in an attempt to discover how wide a sentiment could be marshalled in support of giving the award to you. This got to the Board of Directors, and we finally got an answer that nothing could be done this year because "another man" had already been designated for the current award, and that only one award could be made annually. Through the "grapevine route" we also got word that there were several members of the Board of the Institute who brought up the point that they feared that you might decline an award from the Institute of Architects, and that might prove embarrassing. The Board has to act unanimously on the Gold Medal.

Of course, the Institute of Architects is in many ways a democratic institution and is subject to all the creaking and groaning of the machinery as a result of various kinds of pressure—desirable as well as undesirable. I am sure that all of us have had many reasons to be embarrassed by the discords, but behind it all lie the forces of truth and enlightenment. I think an award to you would be an expression of these better forces, and I have said that I am sure you would recognize it in that light.

I know that you would accept an award if it represented impulses you believe were fine; but I'm sure that you would refuse an award which you felt was prompted by impulses in which you did not believe. This is a correct judgment of you, is it not? What more could you say?

Always sincerely and affectionately,
Arthur C. Holden

April 22, 1948
Mr. Arthur C. Holden
Holden, McLaughlin & Associates
New York City, N.Y.

Dear Arthur:

You are right about my feeling where "recognition" by contemporaries and colleagues is concerned. The only value it could have would be the spirit in which it was given.

I am no cad and would never refuse a token of friendship and esteem sincerely tendered even as an "honor."

December 6, 1948
Mr. Frank Lloyd Wright
Taliesin West, Phoenix, Arizona

Dear Mr. Wright:

It is my singular pleasure and privilege to notify you that by action of The Board of Directors, in semi-annual meeting last week at Sea Island, Georgia, the Gold Medal of The American Institute of Architects was voted for award to you in recognition of most distinguished service to the profession of architecture. It is our sincere hope that you will accept this award and will be present to receive it in person during the Convention of The Institute in Houston, Texas, March 15-18, 1949.

It is customary to make the presentation at the Annual Dinner and the ceremony will be worthy of the honor it symbolizes. The Dinner will be held at the Hotel Rice in Houston on the evening of March seventeenth.

Needless to say, it is most desirable that the award be known to only The Board of Directors and the recipient until we have received your acceptance, at which time a statement will be released by The Institute.

I should like to take this opportunity to proffer my personal felicitations and say that in making this award I feel we honor the profession and The American Institute of Architects.

Would you be good enough to send an early response to me at my office, 96 Grove Street, New Haven 11, Connecticut?

Sincerely yours,
Douglas William Orr, President
The American Institute of Architects

Frank Lloyd Wright, 1949

Frank Lloyd Wright, 1957

Frank Lloyd Wright, 1957

At the Guggenheim Museum, 1959

December 13, 1948
Douglas William Orr, President
The American Institute of Architects
New Haven, Connecticut

My dear President Orr:

I am deeply touched by this token of esteem from the home-boys and assure you that I will attend the Houston convention to say so in person. This token coming, as it does, to one who has constantly remained outside the ranks of the Institute proves me wrong in not having joined that body long ago to work within it for the things I have been consistently working for outside it.

To give the token honorary value I suppose the recipient is freed from all license requirements in our country where the practice of architecture is concerned and anyone working with him, later seeking a license, would be accredited the time so spent as practical experience.

Kindly convey my appreciation to your members. I am glad to be counted as one of you.

January 7, 1949
Mr. Frank Lloyd Wright
Taliesin West, Phoenix, Arizona

Dear Mr. Wright:

Due to a great many meetings and the holiday season my reply to your most gratifying letter of December 13 has been delayed. I was delighted to learn that you will plan to attend the Houston Convention to accept in person the award of The Institute's Gold Medal. I am sure it will be a most stimulating occasion.

It has been the custom in the past for the recipient, in his response, to review his philosophy of architecture and to utilize whatever time he wished in so doing, usually forty to fifty minutes. You may feel free to limit or extend your discourse and I know the members and delegates would look forward to a talk. I would appreciate it if you would advise me, at your convenience, your preference as to the approximate length of time you would like to address the meeting, in order that we may arrange the schedule.

Looking forward to the occasion at Houston.

Sincerely yours,
Douglas William Orr
President

January 15, 1949
Douglas William Orr, President
The American Institute of Architects
Washington, D.C.

My dear Mr. President:

My remarks can be brief or not according to the spirit of the occasion. They will be extemporaneous in any event and can therefore be suited to your plans.

ACCEPTANCE SPEECH OF FRANK LLOYD WRIGHT
Upon Receiving the Gold Medal of the American Institute of
Architects, Rice Hotel, Houston, Texas, March 17, 1949.

LADIES AND GENTLEMEN:

No man climbs so high or sinks so low that he isn't eager to receive the good will and admiration of his fellow man. He may be reprehensible in many ways, he may seem to care nothing about it; he may hitch his wagon to a star and, however he may be circumstanced or whatever his ideals or his actions, he never loses the desire for the approbation of his kind.

So I feel humble and grateful—I don't think humility is a very becoming state for me, but I really feel by this token of esteem from the "home boys"—it has reached me...from almost every great nation in the world—it's been a long time coming from home. But here it is at last, and very handsomely indeed...and I'm extremely grateful. I don't know what change it's going to effect upon my course in future. It's bound to have an effect. I'm not going to be the same man when I walk out of here that I was when I came in. Because, by this little token in my pocket, it seems to me that a *battle has been won*.

I was sitting in my little home in Arizona in '41 when the news came over the wire that the Gold Medal of the Royal Institute of British Architects had fallen to a lad out there in the Middle West in the tall grass. I felt then that the youngsters who have held, we'll say, with me, who have worked with me and who have believed, and made sacrifices, and taken the gaff with me, had won a worldwide fight. But it hadn't been won at home!

(By the way, have any of you observed what we fellows have done to the Colonial? Have you seen it come down and its front open to the weather and the wings extend and have it become more and more reconciled to the ground? It has. You notice it.)

It's very unbecoming on an occasion like this, to boast. But I do want to say something that may account in a measure for the fact that I have not been a member of your professional body, that I have consistently maintained an amateur's status. Long ago, back in the days of Oak Park, I set up a standard of payment for my services of 10 percent. I have consistently maintained it. I have always felt a competition for the services of an architect—who, to me, is a great creative artist—was a sacrilege, a shame, and pointed to history to prove that nothing good ever came of it. And I think nothing good ever will come of it. Also, I think that to make sketches for anybody for nothing, to tender your services, to hawk yourself in the curb in any circumstances is reprehensible. Now I know the ideals of this Institute very well. I took them to heart years ago. And believe me, with this medal in my pocket, I can assert truthfully that never have I sacrificed one iota of those ideals in any connection whatsoever. The man does not live who can say that I sought his work.

I remember in the very early days, when the children were running around the streets without proper shoes, Mr. Moore, across the way, wanted to build a house. A fine house, a fine man, a great opportunity for a youngster like me. I had these ideals at heart, even then. And I never went to see Mr. Moore, I never asked anybody to say a word for me because who was there who could say an honest one? They didn't know anything about me. But I glanced up, one day, through the plate glass door—and, by the way, I started the plate glass door—and there were Mr. and Mrs. Moore! Well, you can imagine how that heart of mine went pitty-pat! They came in and sat down opposite me.

"Now, Mr. Wright," he said, "I want to know why every architect I ever heard of and a great many I never heard of have come to ask me for the job of building my house."

I said, "I can't answer that question. But I am curious to know—did Mr. Patton come?" Mr. Patton was the president of the A.I.A. at that time.

"Why," he said, "He was the first man to come."

"Well now," I said.

Mr. Moore said, "Why haven't *you* come to ask me to build my house—you live right across the road."

I said, "You're a lawyer, aren't you, Mr. Moore? You're a professional man. If you heard that somebody was in trouble, would you go to him and offer him your services?"

"Ah-h," he said. "I thought that was it! You're going to build our house."

It began that way, and it began to get noised about.

The next man was Mr. Baldwin, who was also a lawyer and wanted to build a house. Mr. Baldwin appears several months afterward and lays a check on the table. It wasn't a big check. It was $350 but it would be $3,500 now. And you can imagine what *that* did to me!

And he said, "Here's your retainer, Mr. Wright."

That's how it began, and it's been that way ever since. I've never in my life asked a man to say a good word for me to another man who is going to build. Well now as a consequence I've been sitting around, waiting. I've spent a good many years of my life *hoping* somebody would come and *give* me something to do. And every job I ever had hit me out of the blue on the back of my head. That's true. So this gold medal, let's forget all about design, let's forget all about contributions to construction, and all the rest of it. I feel that I can stick it in my pocket and walk away with it just because I sat there, waiting for a job.

Now, of course, architecture is in the gutter. It is. I've heard myself referred to as a great architect. I've heard myself referred to as the greatest *living* architect. I've heard myself referred to as the greatest architect who ever lived. Now wouldn't you think that ought to *move* you? Well it doesn't. Because in the first place, they don't know. In the next place, no architect in the sense that a man has now to be an architect ever lived, and that's what these boys in front of me here don't seem to know.

Architects as they existed in the ancient times—were in possession of a state of society as an instrument to build with. The guilds were well organized. The predetermined styles were well established—especially in the Gothic period. An architect in those days was pretty well furnished forth with everything he needed to work with. He didn't have to be a creator. He had to be a sentient artist with a fine perception, let's say, and some knowledge of building—especially if he was going to engage in some monumental enterprise. But he didn't have to create—as he does now.

Now we have an entirely different condition. We live by the machine. Most of us aren't much higher in our consciousness and mentality than a man in a garage, anyhow. We *do* live by the machine. We *do* have the great products of science as our toolbox, and as a matter of fact science has ruined us as it has ruined religion, as it has made a monkey of philosophy, as it has practically destroyed us and sent us into perpetual war. Now that isn't our fault. But where—I ask you—were these new forms of building to come from—that could make full use of these advantages that have proved to us so disadvantageous? Who is going to conceive these *new buildings*? Where from? How come?

It's a great pity that the Greeks didn't have glass...great pity that they didn't have steel—spider spinning. Because if they had, we wouldn't have to do any thinking even now. We would copy them with gratitude. No, not with gratitude, we wouldn't even know we were copying them. We would take it all for granted. We wouldn't have the least gratitude.

But now—what must an architect be if he's really going to be one worth while—if he's really going to be *true* to his profession? He must be a creator. He must *perceive* beyond the present. He must see pretty far ahead. He must see into the life of things, if he is going to build anything worth building in this day and generation.

We ought to be the greatest builders the world has ever seen. We have the riches, we have the materials, we have the greatest release—ever found by man—in steel and in glass. We have everything *but*. We have a freedom that never existed before. We profess democracy out of a mobocracy that is shocking, astounding, and arresting. But we have built *nothing* for democracy. We have built *nothing* in the spirit of freedom that has been ours. No. Look at Washington. Look anywhere. You can even go out and see the Shamrock in Houston. And, by the way, I want it recorded right here and now, that that building is built in what is called the International Modern style. Let's give the devil his due. Let's put it where it belongs. And anyhow, while we're speaking of that exploit—why? It ought to be written in front of it in great, tall letters, in electric lights: W-H-Y? *Why?* Well—Houston has it, and Houston is a good example of the capitalist city—the pattern of the capitalist city. One single, great, broad pavement—skyscrapers erected at one end—and way in the country at the other end-skyscraper. In between—out on the prairie and in the mud—the people.

Now we are prosecuting a cold war with people who declare—with a fanatic faith that is pitiful—in the "have-nots." We declare a faith in the "haves"—when we act. We declare a faith in the union, or something beneficial to both the haves and the have-nots—when we talk. Now, when are we going to practice what we preach? When are we going to *build* for democracy? When are we going to understand the significance of the thing ourselves, and live up to it? When are we going to be willing to sit and *wait* for success? When are we going to be willing to take the great will and the great desire for the deed?

We can do it. We've got "enough on the ball," as the slang phrase is, to go on with in that direction, if we will. But to me the most serious lack, the thing we haven't got—and if you look over the political scene, of course, it's *obscene*—of all this thing we're talking about; Honor? Nowhere. Now what is a sense of honor? What would it be in architecture? What would it be in the building of buildings? What would it be in the living of a life? In a democracy—under freedom—not mistaking license for freedom, not mistaking individuality for personality, which is our great error and which characterizes us as a mobocracy instead of a true democracy. What would a sense of honor be—that sense of honor that could save us now? As science has mowed us down—and we're lying ready to be raked over the brink—what could save us but a sense of honor? And what would that sense of honor be? What is the honor of a brick? What would be an honorable brick? A *brick* brick, wouldn't it? A *good* brick. What would be the honor of a board? It would be a *good* board, wouldn't it? What's the honor of a man? To be a *true* individual—to live up to his ideal of individuality rather than his sense of personality. If we get that distinction straight—in our minds—we'll be able to go on. We will last—some—time. If we don't get it, we might as well prepare for the brink; we're going over.

I've been right about a good many things. That's the basis of a good deal of my arrogance. And it has a basis—that's one thing I can say for *my* arrogance. We can save ourselves. We're smart. We have a certain rat-like perspicacity. But we have the same courage, and that's what's the matter. I don't know of a more cowardly...well, I'm getting too deep in here now, and I can't swear—not tonight. But we are certainly a great brand of cowardice in America. We've let all our great opportunities to live a spiritual life with great interior strength and nobility of purpose in mind go by the board. Why—I've asked myself all these years—why? You've all seen it. I'm not telling you anything new. Churches, religion, what has it become? Philosophy— what is it? Education—what have you? Cowardice. What are the universities today? Overflowing with hungry minds and students. And yet—as I stand here now—I'm perfectly willing to admit and to confess that it's not the fault of the universities. It's not the fault of education. None of this is the fault of the systems that exist among us. They're our *own fault. We* make these things what they are. We allow them to be as they are. We've got the kind of buildings we deserve. We've got the kind of cities that're coming to us. This capitalist city, for instance, of which Houston is an example. *We* did it! It came to us because we are what we are—and don't forget it!

If we're ever going to get anything better, if we're ever going to come by a more honorable expression of a civilization such as the world is entitled to from us—we put ourselves on a hill here—in a high light—we talk about the highest standard of living the world has ever seen—we profess all these things—and *we don't deliver.*

It isn't the fault of institutions. It isn't the fault of any class. It isn't the fault of the big boys that make the money and make the blunders and shove us over the brink we spoke of a minute ago. No. How would they *learn* better? How is the architect who built the building going to know any better? How are they going to find out? They can only find out by your disapproval. They can only find out by your telling the *truth,* first to yourselves, and then out loud wherever you can get a chance to tell it.

We've got to find honor. You know the old sayings—we dislike them now because they're a reproach. We don't honor the men who came over with an ideal in their hearts and founded this basis, as they thought, for freedom. They couldn't foresee that by the way of sudden riches and these new scientific powers put into our hands that we would be so soon degenerate.

I think if we were to wake up and take a good look at ourselves, as *ourselves*—without trying to pass the buck—without trying to blame other people for what really is our own shortcoming and our own lack of character we would be an example to the world that the world needs now. We wouldn't be pursuing a cold war. We would be pursuing a great endeavor to plant, rear, and nurture a civilization. And we would have a culture that would convince the whole world. We'd have all the Russians in here on us, working for us—with us—not afraid that we were going to destroy them or destroy anybody else. It's because of cowardice and political chicanery, because of the degradation to which we have fallen—as *men.*

Well now that's serious enough, and that's all that I think I ought to say.

But, I want to call your attention to one thing: I built it. *I have built it.* Therein lies the source of my arrogance—why I can stand here tonight, look you in the face, and insult you. I don't think many of you realize what it is that has happened or is happening in the world, that is now coming toward us.

In a little place where we live with 60 youngsters, we turned away 400 in the past two years and they come from 26 different nations. They all come as volunteers because this thought that we call organic architecture has gone abroad. It has *won* abroad under different names. Singular thing: we will never take an original thought or an idea until we have diluted it—until we have passed it around and given it a good many names. After that takes place, then we can go and we *do* go.

Well, that has happened. This thing has been named different names all over the world. It's come back home—I say come back home advisedly, because here is where it was born, in this cradle, as we're fond of calling it, of liberty. What are we going to do with it? Are we going to let it become a commonplace and shove it into the gutter? Or are we going to really look up to it—use it—honor it? And, believe me, if we do, we have found the centerline of a democracy. Because the principles of an organic architecture, once you comprehend them, naturally grow and expand into this great freedom that we hoped for when we founded this nation and that we call Democracy.